FLYING SMART

Also by Zalin Grant

Survivors
Over the Beach
Facing the Phoenix

FLYING SMART

Zalin Grant

Printed in the United States of America
Cover Design by Archie Delapaz
Design and Composition by Claude Norcott, Vienna, Va

First Edition

Library of Congress Catalog Card Number: 95-74742
Grant, Zalin
Flying Smart/Zalin Grant

ISBN 0-9648736-0-5

Pythia Press
11206 Wedge Drive
Reston, VA 22090

Tel: (703) 709-0919
Fax: (703) 709-1333
E-mail: pythiapres@aol.com

For

Barbara Dean and James David,

my favorite niece and nephew

CONTENTS

INTRODUCTION

During the past thirty years I have flown over a million miles on everything from shot-up helicopters in Vietnam to the gleaming, turtle-waxed airplane used by the President of the United States. My work as a journalist or simple curiosity has taken me to more than eighty countries. I've learned a lot of tricks of traveling in those three decades.

Yet it never occurred to me to set down what I knew about flying smart. Until, that is, my mother suddenly announced that she was coming to Paris to visit me and my wife Claude.

What consternation that caused in our household!

This would be my mother's first trip to Europe. In fact, her first flight to anywhere. She had never stepped on an airplane. And as Claude reminded me, "You are going to be held accountable as her personal navigator. You'd better make it good and true, as Hemingway would have said."

Luckily I knew, my mother was just like me. Or more accurately, I was like her. We both hated surprises. We both figured we could handle most anything that life threw up if only we understood how it really worked.

We had a love of the tiny details. If there was something we didn't know much about, no one could explain it too fully for our taste. I was not inclined to cut someone short by saying, "Hold on, you're insulting my intelligence." More likely my response was, "Hey, let's hear more of that."

She'd want to know every detail about her flight to Paris—that I knew. All the important things. Like how to get in and out of the bathroom. Or where to put her handbaggage. Exactly what to expect from takeoff to landing.

So *Flying Smart* took off at 2:30 p.m., on January 29, 1985. That's when I sat down to organize my notes and to make an audiocassette for my mother.

Her trip was a great success. Not only did she like Paris and love Claude, but she also sprinkled compliments like confetti when she talked about my suggestions for flying smart. Ten years later she was still playing my tape for friends and strangers. Some of them never intended to take an international flight, she told me, but they enjoyed knowing what it was like, anyway.

Early on she suggested that I turn *Flying Smart* into a book. But I had already signed a contract to do another work, and so I reluctantly put aside my notes. Then on a recent flight from Paris to Washington it suddenly hit me. Air travel had changed dramatically in the ten years since I had sat down to advise my mother.

Changed for the worse.

Flying Smart

Air travel had become a truly modern mass transport system. Which meant that it was something to be endured. An ordeal not a pleasure. Gone forever were the days of "Coffee, Tea, or Me."

More people were using the system. From every country around the globe. And more people were flying dumb.

I knew the time had come to write *Flying Smart*. So I began to put down what I had learned about air travel during the past thirty years. My plan was to produce a short book, straightforward and personal, that would work on three levels.

First, readers who had never taken an airplane could learn the procedure from beginning to end.

Second, since so many people were already flying domestic these days, the book would contain tips to make their flying smoother. (I would ask them to skip my discussion of certain matters they were already familiar with—like boarding cards and ticketing.)

Third, the major thrust of *Flying Smart* would be pointed to helping first-timers or seasoned domestic flyers meet the ultimate air challenge: international travel.

And *Flying Smart* would contain a lot of those tiny details that my mother's friends, who never intended to board an aircraft, might like to know.

So here we are. Ten years later. Landing.

Zalin Grant
Paris 1995

PRESS
TRIP OF THE PRESIDENT
Name Zalin Grant
Time-Life 625

Part One

VIỆT-NAM

FRONTERAS
12 AGO 19[illegible]
ENTRADA - A
BARCELONA

Visas

-11-1968
-2-1969
[illegible] thấy
hồi nhập-cư
[illegible] month
date of arrival in
[illegible]ng-Lãnh-Sự

Visas
Départures/Sorties
[illegible]SULAT DE FRANCE
WASHINGTON
[illegible] Nº 125628/87
[illegible] NOV. 1987
DURÉE MAXIMUM
de chaque
SÉJOURS
-90-
jours
UTILISABLE JUSQU'AU
12 Nov/92

[illegible]YEN ĐÌNH THONG
Consul

ETRANGERE

وارد شده ود آرنده
امضاء

Actually, I've felt the m[...] comfortable flying when [...] was wearing a parachut[...] (Author, 1963)

STARTING SMART

If you are left-handed, can stand on your head, and agree to depart at 11:52 p.m. on the night of a full moon, then Uranus Airlines has a terrific bargain of a ticket for you.

No, it's not quite that bad. But it often seems so. The various airlines offer a bewildering array of tickets for flying overseas or domestic. Cheap ones. Expensive ones. Prices based on how long you are going to stay, on whether or not you purchase the ticket in advance. Prices based on when you plan to return, even on the particular season of the year. And the deals seem to change with the speed of light.

I don't buy my tickets directly from the airlines. I use a travel agent to help guide me through the maze of prices and conditions. If you want to make your trip easier from the start, you will too.

TRAVEL AGENT

What Makes a *Good* Travel Agency?

The staff is courteous and helpful. Naturally. They don't stay in business very long if they aren't. But I look for more subtle signs and omens.

For instance, I like to watch the way a travel agent plays the computer. Is the agent smooth and fast? Or bumbling and hesitant? There are thousands of flights, thousands of connections to be made, many different kinds of tickets out there—and the computer is the key to your successful booking.

It's reassuring when I find an agile mind that works in harmony with the microprocessor. If I don't, I'll move on.

Easy Flyer

A good travel agent understands that your romantic adventure begins when you land, not when you takeoff. My agents—The Travel Store in Reston, Virginia—try to make the flying experience as easy as they can for their clients.

Example: Along with the ticket, they give me a computer printout of my itinerary. It's on a letter-size piece of paper.

It tells me the name of the airline I'm using, the flight number, the time of departure and arrival. Both going and coming.

That's easier than looking at the small confusing print of the ticket itself. And I can make a photocopy for my friends or family so they know my schedule.

A good travel agent will also, when the air carrier allows it, book your seat in advance and provide you with a boarding pass. More on this later.

How to Find a Travel Agent

Word of mouth is best. Do you have a friend who has taken a trip lately? Ask, and ask again. If you must resort to the yellow pages, look for travel agencies that are accredited to their national association.

Your Obligations

Travel agencies make their money on small commissions from the airlines. It doesn't cost you anything. (Although some air carriers are cutting back on commissions, which means the charge may be passed on the consumer.) But like many businesses they depend on rapid turnover.

Travel agents cannot afford to spend an excessive amount of time with any one client. And of course they aren't overjoyed to see clients who can't make up their minds. Or who want to change their tickets after the deal is done.

Before you call or walk into a travel office, you should have a definite outline for your trip. When do you want to leave? How long do you want to stay? Will you take a restrictive ticket (non-refundable, non-changeable) to get a cheaper price? Then let the travel agent help you fill in the blanks.

If you are handy with a computer and know your way around the Internet, you can avoid the travel agent all together and find the best deals for yourself. However, if you are not an experienced overseas traveler, you might want to check out your itinerary with an agent the first couple of times before you start winging it alone.

Travel agents complain that some clients seem unable to grasp the fact that they need more than a driver's license and two pieces of identification to enter another country. You need a...

PASSPORT

U.S. passports have gone the way of candy bars since I got my first one thirty years ago. They've become smaller, more expensive, and less tasteful.

The current U.S. passport is a 24-page blue booklet. On the inside cover page is the passport number, your photo, and your date and place of birth. The first five pages are devoted to "Important Information" and "Tips for Travelers." The remaining pages are left blank to accommodate visas and entry and exit stamps.

At this writing a passport costs $55 (or $85 if you want it "expedited"). It's valid for ten years.

When Should You Apply for a Passport?

If you plan to travel abroad in the next year or so, you should apply for a passport right now. If your trip is already scheduled, you are behind the curve. You can't be too early when dealing with a bureaucracy. The passport office, by the way, is run by the U.S. State Department.

Leaving in a Hurry

In certain cases you can get a passport within a day or two, even within a few hours if you have an urgency. A lot depends upon which passport office you are using. But you must show up with the required documentation. To get an expedited passport at the main Washington office, for example, you are asked to produce an airline ticket showing your departure date, in addition to the other required information.

Expedited Passport

I recently renewed my passport in Washington, D.C. Because I was leaving soon, I asked to have it expedited. Here's what thirty bucks extra got me.

First, I filled out the required form. Then I stood in the line marked "Information" for forty-five minutes. The clerk in the information booth examined my form and made sure I had two passport photos, and gave me a number.

I waited three hours for my number to come up. The clerk in the passport booth examined my form. She took my photos. Demanded exactly $85 by check or cash. And told me to come back the next day.

The next day I stood in line again for a long time. (The "will call" window was closed, without explanation.) Two people ahead of me were told that their new passports had been lost. They would have to start over. The clerk's attitude: Tough luck.

Maybe it was just an off day for the passport office. But you get the picture, I believe.

What's Required for Your First Passport?

You must apply in person if you are 13 or older. And you must have a certified copy of your birth certificate. What? Yes, a birth certificate. Usually, you apply for a birth certificate at your city hall or county offices, where the

Recorder of Deeds and so forth are located. If you don't have a birth certificate, you had better have a good reason and show up with a hospital birth record, school records and such, plus a notarized affidavit by an older blood relative who has personal knowledge of your birth.

If you were born abroad, you need a Certificate of Naturalization, Certificate of Citizenship, Report of Birth Abroad of U.S. Citizens. If you can't produce these, ask the State Department official for other alternatives.

Where to Apply for a Passport

In the United States over 2500 courts and 900 post offices accept passport applications. Passport agencies are also located in 13 major cities—Boston, Chicago, Honolulu, Houston, Los Angeles, Miami, New Orleans, New York, Philadelphia, San Francisco, Seattle, Stamford CT, and Washington, D.C. There's bound to be an accepting office close to you, so ask around. The main office is located at:

Washington Passport Agency
1111 19th Street N.W.
Washington, D.C. 20522-1705.

You can phone their information number and get one of those recorded voices that tell you to push such-and-such button for such-and-such information.

Besides the birth certificate, you need to fill out a form and present two passport photos. The two passport photos are no big deal, just a head-and-shoulders shot like on your driver's license. But a couple of tips:

1. The two photos must be precisely the size and type required by the passport office (2x2 inches). Therefore, it's better to get your photos made at a shop that clearly advertises "passport photos."

2. You'll be looking at your picture for the next ten years. You might want to comb your hair and ask the photographer to give you a choice of shots.

If you already have a passport, you can renew it in person or by mail. I renew mine four to six months in advance of its expiration date—not at the last minute, mind you.

Lost or Stolen Passports

I had never had a passport lost or stolen, until I began to write this book. Claude walked out of a Paris bank one day at noon, carrying a small briefcase containing 1,000 francs ($200) and all my old passports, which she was on the way to have photographed to use in *Flying Smart*. Two guys on a motorbike pulled up behind, pushed her down, and stole the briefcase.

Street thieves usually dump everything but valuables quite quickly, so on the off-chance that somebody had found and sent my old passports to the U.S. Embassy, I phoned one morning some days later. First of all, I could only get through to a machine giving out information about what to do in the case of stolen or lost passports. But the machine was talking about current passports, which didn't apply to me. Finally, I was able to explain my problem to a woman at the general information number.

She said, "I know you want to talk to a human being. But that's impossible until after three in the afternoon. They don't take calls in the morning."

Now I'm not one of those people who rail against the government—at least, not more than once or twice a week. But this is what you will be up against if you lose your passport. It will ruin your vacation. And too many people lose or have their passports stolen out of simple carelessness. Believe me, you don't want to hassle your way through the bureaucracy, so be careful with your passport.

Of course there are times, as in Claude's incident, where loss cannot be avoided. If it happens to you, I recommend that you show up in person at nine a.m. at the nearest U.S. Consulate. You must have with you two American-size passport photos. That is, you can't walk into a passport photo shop overseas and tell them you want two photos. They'll give you photos of that country's size, not ours. So you must specify that the photos are 5 by 5 centimeters—that's 2 by 2 inches.

You also must have any and all kinds of identification you can muster to prove you are who you say you are. The embassies ask that you provide a certified copy of your birth certificate. Which is silly. Who travels with a birth certificate? A driver's license and credit cards will suffice in most cases. If all your ID has been lost or stolen, show up with an American citizen who can vouch for you. The U.S. Embassy in Paris says it needs at least one hour to process an application. I think we can safely bet that you'll be there longer.

DO YOU NEED A VISA?

Everybody needs a passport to enter an overseas country. But you may need something more. A visa. This doesn't apply if you are visiting a country in Western Europe. England or France, for example. There, a visa will be accorded you automatically for three months when you show your U.S. passport at immigration. But some other countries require a visa that you must obtain before you enter their borders.

What's a Visa?

Dictionary definition: "An endorsement made on a passport by the proper authorities, denoting that it has been examined, and that the bearer may proceed."

In short, it's just a stamp in your passport. But, sometimes, getting one can be a hassle. A rule of thumb I've developed in my travels: The less important the country, the larger its visa stamp...and the more expensive...and the more troublesome to obtain.

How Do You Obtain a Visa?

By applying to the country's embassy or consulate in Washington or New York or wherever it has one. In some cases, you fill out a form and show them your passport. Other times, a couple of photos are also required. The process may take a long time, so start early.

How Do You Know Whether You Need a Visa?

Ask your travel agent. Or you can call the State Department for recorded information about any country in the world, to learn whether a visa is required and whether certain medical inoculations are needed for entry. If you want to be extra sure, phone the country's embassy in Washington. But don't leave home without one. Remember...

THEIR LAWS ARE YOUR LAWS

A U.S. passport confers no immunity or special privilege. If you visit another country you fall under that country's laws. Stamping your foot and saying "I'm an American citizen" will get you nowhere if you are caught violating the law. And you shouldn't count on the U.S. embassy to save your bean bag if you do something wrong.

Some of their laws you might not agree with. A small Asian country that I generally admire banned chewing gum, for example. That seemed to me a mite excessive. But you can bet I wasn't chewing gum when I entered that country.

Don't Be a Pigeon

In the days before faxes and modems and satellites, journalists working overseas often relied on what we called "pigeons" (as in carrier pigeon) to ferry their articles, packages, and film to the United States. We'd rush out to the airport, spot a likely-looking American tourist, and ask him or her to carry our stuff back to the States, where they would be met at the airport by someone from our local office.

Flying Smart

I was always impressed by the generosity of American tourists. I was never turned down a single time. And on my trips back home I often served as a pigeon too. But then in those days, I also picked up hitchhikers.

Times have changed. The world has grown more dangerous and unpredictable. Do not agree to carry anything for anyone you have not personally and closely known for a long time. And then make sure you thoroughly examine what you have been asked to carry.

A Holiday Romance Is Not Knowing Someone

Young women are particularly susceptible to this scam. They meet Mr. Sincere, look deeply into his soulful eyes, have a brief affair—and honestly believe that they really know him. When the woman is about to depart for home, he asks her to carry something for him.

And what does she do?

She winds up in jail. The package or bag Mr. Sincere sweet-talked her into carrying contains drugs or, in some cases, even a terrorist bomb.

She has never done anything wrong in her life. She's shocked to find that the police don't believe—or disbelieve—her story. They don't care. And this country doesn't have habeas corpus or even bail. The American diplomat from the U.S. embassy who tells her not to worry looks worried himself. She languishes in jail for years, despite the efforts of her family and the State Department to free her.

Well, okay, enough. Don't be a pigeon.

Another way Americans sometimes get themselves into trouble is by violating a country's currency regulations. It once happened to me in a rather odd way—and I'm still kicking myself.

I was coming through Checkpoint Charlie from East Germany in the days before the Berlin Wall fell. The East Germans had demanded that I purchase a certain amount of their currency when I went in. When I started to leave they told me I couldn't take any of their ostmarks with me. Either I had to turn around and go back to spend it. Or I had to donate the cash to a charity which I suspected was themselves.

Impulsively, I pulled the ostmarks from my pocket—the equivalent of less than twenty dollars—and tore them up.

"There," I said, "I think that takes care of the problem."

It didn't.

I was immediately surrounded by armed guards. Destroying their currency was seriously against the law. Only with a great deal of nervous persuasion—and perhaps because I was a journalist—was I able to talk my way out of that one.

Which reminds me. I should tell you about changing money for your trip.

MONEY SMART

Not long ago I passed an American who stood at the money change window at a Paris airport. He was red-faced, the veins on his forehead bulged, and he was yelling, "You are trying to rip me off!"

Uh-huh, I thought. Another one. The guy looked like he was headed to heart-attack city. Or certainly he was off to a bad start on his vacation. Simply because he didn't understand how the currency exchange system works.

The American appeared to be a college-educated type who had checked his newspaper to see what the exchange rate was between the dollar and the franc. And he was angered to find that the rate he was given at the airport didn't correspond to the rate he had read in the *Times* or the *Post*.

It never does.

The dollar exchange rates that you see in the paper or on CNN are based on the trillion-dollar-a-day international currency market. If you've got a million dollars to change for a foreign currency at a single stroke, then you might get a rate approaching the rate you read in the paper. But even a million dollars is not considered much on the international market.

The exchange rate that you receive as a tourist will be lower than the rate you read in the paper. Moreover, the rate at the airport is usually less than you can get at a bank in town.

In Europe the airport rate isn't significantly lower and won't make much difference, unless you are changing a great deal of money. But be careful. In many third world countries the airport rate can vary as much as minus 15% to 20% to the rate you can get at a bank in town.

And you've got to be on guard for hyper-inflation if the country you are visiting has a shaky economy. Some currencies fall by fifteen percent or more *daily*. This means you want to change small sums every day or so in order to keep from losing your purchasing power.

If you see a money change kiosk in town that looks like a genuine commercial enterprise and clearly states its exchange rates out front, you can assume that it's regulated—either by the government or by market forces. But check the rates at several more kiosks to make sure.

So I could have assured the angry American that he had entered a relatively classless exchange rate society: we all get ripped off about the same.

By Credit Card Too

You have probably seen the advertisement of an American tourist putting his credit card in an automatic teller machine in a foreign city, punching in his PIN—and out slides the amount of foreign currency he requested. Easy as pie.

Sure, that works in many places around the world now, especially in Western Europe, if you carry major plastic such as Visa or MasterCard. ATMs are increasing every day.

What they don't tell you, though, is that the credit card company charges you a fee for making the exchange. *Plus* gives you an exchange rate against the dollar that could be less than you can find on the street for cash or travelers check. The credit card guys say that their exchange rates give you the best deal. But, as you know, they also think their monthly interest charges are very reasonable.

If you are running on a tight budget and plan to use your plastic overseas, I recommend that you check with your credit card representative before leaving the States. First, to make sure it's usable where you are going. Second, to get an idea how much you will be losing on every hundred dollars changed.

The Blackmarket

A currency blackmarket exists in some of the lesser developed countries around the world. These countries have a shaky government and/or a shaky economy. Their money does not inspire trust.

The government establishes an official exchange rate at, say, 10-to-1 to the dollar. It requires banks to change money at that rate. Then inflation or a lack of confidence in the country's economy sets in.

A blackmarket springs up. Illegal dealers on the street will give you 15-to-1 for your dollar, instead of the official ten to one.

The government, desperate to protect its money and to garner hard currency dollars at an advantageous exchange rate, refuses to change the official rate to the more realistic rate set by the complex market forces that have created the blackmarket.

Suddenly someone steps out of an alley and offers you 25-to-1 for your dollar. Hey, the blackmarket rate looks very tempting, doesn't it? But remember, it's illegal.

I am not going to tell you I've changed money on the blackmarket. On the other hand, I'll not tell you I haven't. Let's just say that I know a little about the subject.

The governments of countries where blackmarkets exist realize that the blackmarket rate represents the realistic world rate. (How foreign exchange rates are precisely determined, I don't know. If you find out let me know and we'll make a fortune.) Some of the government officials are probably changing money on the blackmarket themselves.

Nevertheless the police can use your participation in the blackmarket as an excuse to give you a big fine or throw you in jail. I know people that has happened to. Some of them were very bright in school—but stupid enough on the streets to sign a personal check to change on the blackmarket.

Besides that, there's the old-as-the-hills money-change scam run by crooks from one end of the globe to the other. The scammer sees you on the street. He pulls you into an alley and offers you a very high rate. "It's dangerous," he says. "We must do it quick."

Then he counts with a thumb flick a stack of banknotes, tied with a string or rubber band. Real currency is on the top and bottom. Blank paper or smaller banknotes are inside the stack. The guy leaves in a flash—and you've just learned a costly lesson.

Watch the Value Added Tax

Countries in Western Europe add a tax on many goods and services. That shouldn't surprise you. But the size of the tax might. It ranges from 6.5% in Switzerland to 25% in Sweden. It's around 20% in England and France. Sometimes the VAT is not included in the advertised price. Before buying ask, "What is the final price with tax?"

If you purchase certain big ticket items, you may—or may not—get a refund of the valued added tax at the airport before you leave. It depends on the country. In theory they are supposed to refund the tax if you are a tourist. But some of the countries make it as difficult as possible for you, hoping the red tape will overwhelm you.

The last time I bought some electronic gear in London the shopkeepers told me they would mail me the tax refund if I would send them proof stamped by immigration that I had left the country. Which I did. They were surprised three months later, when I showed up and demanded my money that hadn't arrived. In any case, have a talk with your hotel staff and learn the procedure for getting a refund of the VAT in the particular country you are visiting.

What's the Money Smart Way?

It depends on your financial situation and how closely you watch the pennies. But here are a few general principles everyone can follow to be money smart:

1. Try to change enough money before you leave the United States to get you from the airport to the hotel on your arrival. This can be done at many big banks located in American cities. Ask for small bills.

2. If you can't change any money before you leave, then change the minimum amount at the airport that you need for transportation to reach your hotel.

3. When you reach the hotel ask the deskperson for information on the best place to change money.

4. The best rate is almost always to be found at an established bank that has a bureau of exchange. Not all of them do. So check and then make sure you are standing in the right line. And ask yourself: Is the time spent going to a real bank worth the amount gained over the time saved going to a convenient money change office for tourists?

5. Carry a hand calculator to help you convert sums of an unfamiliar currency into dollars and vice versa.

6. Change only the amount you estimate that you'll need. Or change your money several times as you run low. Reason: When you return to the money changer to repurchase dollars with a foreign currency at the trip's conclusion, you'll get a lower exchange rate on that end too. Yep. As the angry American might have said, ripped off again.

WHEN TO FLY

Friday the 13th. That's when many airlines experience a sudden drop of customers. Which leaves you with a spacious airplane and many seats to choose from.

Okay, I'm kidding a bit. If you happen to be superstitious yourself, you might want to consider several alternate days when passenger traffic is often low—Tuesday, Wednesday or Thursday. I usually fly on Thursdays.

What you want to avoid, of course, if possible, is flying on a weekend. Especially during tourist season. Then you'll probably have as much spread room as a sardine. If you must travel on a weekend, then flying smart becomes all the more imperative.

Zalin Grant

ARE YOU AFRAID?

I am. To be trapped in a metal tube six miles above the earth is not a natural experience for a primate. After hundreds of flights I still get a flutter when that thing leaves the ground. Anybody who tells me they aren't bothered in the least does not, in my opinion, have a proper appreciation of what can go wrong. More to the point, I think they're a little—well, *nuts.*

Airline studies report that between sixty and seventy percent of all passengers experience an emotion ranging from slight uneasiness to sheer panic. So you and I aren't alone. Some airlines (including American Airlines and Air France) offer, for a price, an anti-fright flight program. Then there are a number of things that you can personally do to lower your fright factor.

During my five years as a war correspondent, I learned that FDR's famous declaration that "We have nothing to fear but fear itself" is not really true, except in the situation he described. Fear is natural. You simply have to know how to manage it.

I'll speak more about this later. But let's hit the big thing you can do, right now. Which is: You must concentrate on lowering stress and minimizing jet lag by being smart about everything under your control.

You can't fly the airplane. But you can do a lot to put your mind and body in the best possible shape for the flight. And you start by watching what you eat.

EATING SMART

On the day of my most recent flight to Europe I ate only a grilled cheese sandwich and a chocolate shake before I left. After arriving in Paris I stuffed myself with a couscous, topped off with peppery harissa, accompanied by a white wine.

In between I consumed nothing but Evian water.

Being stuck in an airplane for long hours does weird things to your body. So your physical preparation for the trip must begin before you actually step on the aircraft. Besides adding comfort to your flight, eating smart may determine how well and fast your internal clock adjusts to your new time zone. Which in turn will influence how much you enjoy your trip.

Theories abound about how to handle this problem. Some people swear by the feast-and-fast strategy. Three days before departure, they say, eat high-protein and high-carbohydrate foods, breakfast and lunch. Two days before, eat lightly. The day before, feast again. Then departure day, eat lightly.

The feast-and-fast strategy posits that the light-food days reduce the amount of carbohydrates in the liver and therefore allows the body to adjust more easily to its new time zone.

I don't really understand it myself. But there is one thing I know from long experience:

Unless you've got an extraordinary Rolls-Royce of a digestive system, you'd better watch what you eat and drink for several days leading up to the flight—and on the flight itself.

You Know Your Body Best

I like Tex-Mex, Sichuan, Sri Lanka curry and many other of the world's spice of foods. And I've had no digestive problems since the bug got me on my first trip to Asia.

But something bland, like a grilled cheese sandwich and a chocolate milkshake, works best for me before a flight. It cuts my appetite, sits well, and allows me to move easily into my new time zone meal schedule.

You know what works best for you. Maybe a salad. Tuna fish. A little non-acidic fruit. Just keep it light.

Eating Smart Takes Social Discipline

One of the biggest problems in maintaining a proper pre-flight diet is the friends-and-family factor. They often want to take you out for a celebratory or goodbye meal before your trip abroad.

This happened to me on my departure day. My friends invited me to a farewell lunch at a restaurant. Naturally, they were a little disappointed when I ordered only a lowly grilled cheese. They were sophisticated people who flew often but usually on domestic flights.

To hop a two or three hour domestic flight is not the same as spending seven to fifteen hours on an international flight. Not the same at all, remember.

Be Polite But Strong

If someone invites you to a pre-trip dinner or lunch, try to schedule it two or more days before your flight. If you can't, explain that you are eating smart and won't be eating much. You cannot completely beat jet lag. But you can give it a good fight.

WHAT IS JET LAG?

There is really no firm definition. It's a feeling of malaise, of your body being off-kilter, of a slight dizziness behind your eyes. In extreme forms you might have a vague feeling of unreality in your new setting. And days later, when your mind has adjusted to the new environment, your body might still insistently wake up and get hungry based on the hours of your old time zone.

It's easier on jet lag to fly from east to west. That is, from Europe or Asia to the U.S. You gain hours instead of losing them. Sunlight, or the lack of it, is obviously a determinant in the problem. If you are flying home to the U.S., wear dark shades and avoid direct sunlight when you arrive. Then return to your normal scheduled hour to go to bed.

An anti-jet lag pill has been tested on flight crews for the past several years and seems to work without side effects. Melatonin also has shown promise for helping relieve the symptoms of jet lag. But until somebody comes up with the silver bullet, you'll have to follow the guidelines which we know help.

The signs of jet lag are general. But the specifics vary from individual to individual. I find my jet lag getting worse as

I grow older. Some of my friends, when I pick them up at the airport, cheerfully say they feel wonderful and aren't suffering from it the least bit. Then I notice that hollow look in their eyes and realize they are telling their host a polite little lie.

PACKING SMART

I don't. And this has caused me lots of grief. I'm a throw-it-all-in-the-suitcase kind of guy. It's sort of a genetic defect like color blindness. After all these years I still can't figure what to take and what to leave behind.

(A flight attendant I know says: *"I have a theory that many people who over pack lack self-confidence. They want to carry as much as possible to recreate 'a small home' in their hotel room—lots of familiar clothes, family pictures on the bedside table, etc."*)

Hmm. Could that be me? Or do I simply fall into the category of an unredeemed packaholic?

Whatever the cause, I'm the butt of jokes among my friends. How can a guy so savvy about traveling be so dumb about packing, they laugh. But besides the jokes and the back pain there's a darker side to my packing defect.

Trouble at the airport.

I've had to pay outrageous sums to cover my excess weight charges. And you can't argue with the check-in people once they decide you're overweight.

Once, when I was without cash, I was forced to go through my suitcase to discard underpants and shirts and what-have-you, to meet the weight limit. Right in front of other people waiting to check their luggage. Luckily a friend was with me to recover the discards. But it was still an embarrassing experience. And unnecessary.

What Do the Airlines Allow?

It depends on the airline, even the time of year, so you've got to check with the travel agent to find out what is permissible. There's some flexibility if several airlines fly the same route. It's part of their marketing strategy to attract customers.

Carry On

A common dispute at an airport turns on the amount of baggage you can personally carry on the aircraft. Federal Aviation Administration regulations currently limit carry-on bags to two pieces. This doesn't include purses, cameras or umbrellas.

The two pieces of carry-on must be stowed under the seat directly in front of you and/or in the flip-open bin above your head. To fit under a typical airline seat the bag on the floor should be no more than 9 inches by 14 inches by 22 inches. The bag in the overhead rack: no more than 4 by 32 by 45.

Some foreign airlines will allow only one carry-on bag. Another carrier might look the other way if you arrive with three. Or won't count a briefcase in the limitation. You'd better check before leaving. The airlines are getting tougher, not easier, on this matter. You cannot board an aircraft carrying what you would like to carry.

Flying Smart

Check-in Luggage

Checking luggage for an international flight is not the same as checking bags for a domestic flight. On domestic flights you are often given a leeway on weight and number of bags.

But baggage weight on a long flight influences fuel consumption, therefore profitability for the airline. We're talking about their bottom line. That's why they may call you on it if you have excess weight—not for space reasons.

Pack Only What You Really Need

My mother arrived in Paris with a change of clothes for every day. (I realized then my packing defect was hereditary.) That's sort of the American way, I guess. But it is not anybody else's way. People in other countries wear the same clothes over and over.

Besides, the shift to a more casual way of dressing is a worldwide trend. What was considered informal when I was a kid is now considered formal. If you are a guy with a blue blazer or a tweed jacket and a sedate tie, you can get into practically anything short of the king's coronation. And a simple black dress is still a winner for a woman in the evening.

After that you need only a change or two of comfortable clothes, a sweater or jacket for the unpredictable cool nights, and your toilet articles. The head-to-toe method (start at the top and move down by body sections) of packing will help keep you from forgetting something.

To do it right, study the weather conditions and dress codes in a guide book or on the Internet for the country you are visiting, to get an idea of what you should take.

You know what you need for your bathroom routine. But let me suggest one addition that will have a great psychological value—your personal washcloth. Put it in a Ziploc bag so you can move it easily when it's still wet. A bar of your preferred soap should go along with it.

Don't take too many shoes. They bulk up your suitcase and add weight. A pair of presentable shoes, along with a pair of comfortable walking shoes, will do you fine.

Electrical Gear

Airlines are putting more restrictions on the kinds of electronics that can be brought aboard the plane. Pilots complain that some electrical stuff interferes with their navigation system. There's also a worry about somebody smuggling in a terrorist bomb in a tape cassette or radio.

Beyond that, you have another problem. Anything you own that operates with an electrical cord probably won't work overseas. Won't work, that is, unless you have a travel converter *and* a converter plug.

The United States operates on a 110 volt electrical system. Most other countries operate on a 220 volt electrical system. Why? Beats me. (Some Caribbean and Latin American countries use 110V.) We also use a different plug from most other countries.

A Transformer

You must make the conversion between the two currents with a transformer-type converter. To use a transformer, if it's only a hair drier or something requiring DC (direct) current, doesn't present much of a problem.

But if you have electrical gear that contains a motor, your converter transformer must be more sophisticated. I've burned out a couple of American-made electric typewriters by trying to use them overseas with transformers. (A laptop computer, on the other hand, usually comes with an automatic electrical adaptor and presents no problem, except that you must carry a plug-in adaptor if you are using it off-battery.)

My advice is to carry nothing that isn't battery-powered. Except for maybe a hair drier, which pulls a lot of current. But you can buy a travel hair drier that can be shifted between 110V and 220V by flipping a switch or turning a slot with a coin.

Plug Converter

If you plan to take a hair drier, or anything else with a cord, you also need a plug converter to make it work. There are at least four different types of plugs used around the world. The plug for France, for example, has two round prongs, not two flat ones, as we have in the United States.

Where to Find Transformers and Plug Converters

They can usually be found in a good hardware or a shop that specializes in electrical supplies. The plug converter is simple and inexpensive—you plug your plug into it. But you'll waste a lot of time trying to find one if you wait till you reach your travel destination.

In the carry-on bag that you plan to stow beneath the seat in front, leave enough space for the things you might need during the flight. Such as toothbrush and toothpaste, a half-bottle of water, tampons, aspirin or other medicine. Also leave enough space for crucial elements such as passport, tickets and money. Things that you will not let out of your sight the entire trip. Ugly as I find them to be, a security wallet is a very good idea for trip.

Needless to say, you should never pack any valuables in your check-in luggage. Or maybe it's not needless say, since people still do it and get robbed more than the airlines would like to admit. You've got to keep your hands on your stuff. I can't count the times I've been in U.S. consulates around the world and seen American tourists with that stunned look on their faces that told me they'd just lost their valuables and passport to a pick-pocket.

When you finish packing and suddenly realize you've got an awful lot of stuff, I recommend that you set aside enough money to pay the excess weight charges if the airline calls you on it. Either that or do a little repacking. The point is, you've got to check on your airline's over-weight policies because they vary with routes and airports.

Actually I've done much better since my wife Claude invented a twelve-step program for recovering packaholics. (Step One: Pack Smart; Step Two: Pack Smart; etc.)

No, you might have guessed the truth. Claude packs my bags for me. On the other hand, she has trouble finding her car keys. That's our trade-off at home.

SIGNATURE LUGGAGE

I mark my suitcase and bags with colored plastic tape before leaving for the airport. Sometimes I create a design unlikely to be duplicated by anybody else. Other times I just tape the first initial of my unusual first name in a large block on the side. And of course I put a tag with my name and telephone number on the grip as further protection in case the bag gets misrouted. (For extra security, put a tag with your name and address *inside* your luggage.)

The idea is to turn my luggage into an individual piece that stands out brilliantly, as it joins dozens of similar-looking bags on the baggage carrousel after the flight. Something I can spot immediately.

Obviously this works to your advantage in terms of saving time. Once you spot your bag, you can move up the line and retrieve it, always checking your baggage claim ticket to make sure it is really yours.

But I've found that signature luggage can be important in another way. Take, for instance, what happened to me not long ago.

The baggage carrousel area was tightly packed with people and carts. I managed to wedge myself half way down the line from the place where the bags came clanking out. I didn't have a good vantage point. But I was able to spot my suitcase quickly, because it had a large Z taped on both sides.

As I waited for my suitcase to reach me a man suddenly grabbed it and headed for the door. I chased him down and told him that he had made a mistake. At first he argued with me. But then he apologized with great emotion when I showed him my baggage claim.

After talking to the gentleman, who was from another country, I realized that he'd honestly believed there was only one piece of gray Samsonite in the world—and that it belonged to him. He thought the baggage handlers had slapped on the taped Z.

Sure, it may look a bit tacky to mark up your luggage. But the tape or ribbons or sticker can be removed after your flight. With so many similar-looking bags on the pick-up line, and so many first-timers now flying from all over the globe, what can I say but...better tacky than sorry. Cabin crews from airlines all over the world do it; they must know something.

Travelers used to choose flashy and expensive luggage. I guess some still do. But I'm seeing less of it these days. Most people now seem to buy their luggage based on whether it is durable, lightweight, and rollable.

Roll On

Choosing luggage with wheels is well worth the extra cost. When you exit some airports you start to feel like you are on a long desert walk. London's Heathrow, for example. Unless you are a weightlifter or a masochist, I suggest that you go with the wheels, either on the luggage itself or as a collapsible cart.

Flying Smart

In the interest of protecting what you have inside, a rigid bag is better than canvas or other material. Have you ever had a private showing of baggage going from check-in to plane? There's many a slip between cup and lip, I can assure you.

FLYING WITH CLASS

I've flown everything from rumpled charter to luxurious first-class. What do I fly now? Economy, also referred to as Coach.

Occasionally with a little help from my friends, I am upgraded to first-class at no extra charge. And I don't turn it down. On a long flight it's a joy to be able to stretch out on the more comfortable seats of first-class. Not to worry about crowded bathrooms. To be showered with attention by flight attendants.

(Tip: If you are angling for an upgrade, watch how you dress. Many airlines aren't partial to putting sweats and sneakers in their first-class cabin.)

But is it worth the cost difference between a first-class ticket and coach? I don't think so. It might be for you. If you feel no twinge about the price and believe the comfort is worth it. Or if you are making a once-in-a-lifetime trip. First-class could be the way for you to go.

However, I've also had some not-so-good first-class flights. Like the times when I've been trapped in the relatively small space of the first-class cabin with an annoying loudmouth. Some people think having money excuses bad manners.

All things considered, I've settled on flying in the economy or coach section. Which makes every aspect of flying smart even more important.

So having controlled my pre-flight diet and fought off the impulse to pack too much, I now apply the same determination as I start to leave for the airport.

DRESS SMART

I like to shower and use the bathroom in the hour before I leave for the airport. Not only for the hygienics involved but because a little quiet time in the shower has a tranquillizing effect. It's another step in managing stress. Of course a shower is a personal choice. You might find that a long bath has a more soothing effect. Whatever your preference, try to set aside the time before departure.

After showering I carefully choose what I am going to wear on the flight.

What to Wear

Comfort is the key, not fashion or style. But comfort and style are not necessarily incompatible. You don't have to wear sweats and sneakers in order to dress smart for flying.

Nothing Tight

To dress smart simply means that you wear nothing tight. Especially nothing that constricts the stomach, upper torso, neck, and lower body.

For women this means no panty girdles, tight bras or skirts, even panty hose. If you are partial to stockings, try thigh-highs—something you can easily remove in the lavatory after takeoff and replace before landing. A pair of loose-fitting slacks works best of all.

For men this is not the time to squeeze into those pants you keep wearing because you intend to lose weight. If you have to suck in your stomach they're the wrong ones. Pants with a stretch waist are best. A necktie doesn't work either. So be prepared to take it off. Better still, have the tie neatly folded in your carry-on under the seat and ready to put on before landing.

The best fabric for flying is 100% cotton. Synthetic materials tend to warm up by body friction. Cotton reacts to the body like a natural thermostat.

After I reluctantly took off my new but tight Kenzo dress shirt and replaced it with a well-worn Banana Republic casual, I was ready to head to the airport. And I was determined to be on time.

WHAT DOES ON-TIME MEAN?

Wally and Janice Terry, whom I've known since way back when, took me to the airport for my recent flight to Europe. Wally is a journalist and writer who flies a lot. Not by accident, he lives only ten minutes away from the Washington Dulles airport.

Wally met my request to leave for the airport a full two hours in advance with a little humorous exasperation. "Hey, that's why I'm living here, guy! You can't possibly be late." Nevertheless, I insisted.

The airlines ask you to show up two hours before your international flight is scheduled to leave. That's not necessary, of course. They will check you in and put you aboard within minutes of departure time, if they have not made the "final boarding" call on the public address system and closed the aircraft door.

But there are several good reasons for arriving early.

An international flight, especially during tourist season, usually means a lot of people. Lots of people means long lines. And lots of baggage to be checked. Besides avoiding the lines, you want to give your bags a convenient amount of time to find their way to the same flight you are taking.

Flying Smart

Stress Management

Even more important, arriving early at the airport will get you off to a good start on stress management. People who zoom up at the last minute already have their energy force working in a negative way. The nerve endings are tingling, the heart is pumping harder, the armpits are wet. From there it's all down hill.

Knowing When to Leave

When you are in a strange city, with unfamiliar traffic patterns, it's difficult to know when to leave for the airport in order to meet your two-hour-in-advance deadline. My rule of thumb is to ask the hotel deskperson or a taxi driver, and then add a half hour to what they tell me. If I'm taking a bus I take the one just before the one people recommend that I take.

This means that I spend a little more time than necessary at the airport. But when I see fellow passengers rushing in at the last moment, with that half-dazed look on their faces, the adrenaline spurting from their ears, I know that it was worth it. They are not flying smart.

Part Two

EMBASSY, RAWALPINDI
-3 JUL
HEATHROW (3)
KONG
date here
valid.
TOURIST
Visa exemption [illegible] upto 25-9-68
Registration with Police necessary if
stay exceeds three months.
Da[illegible]
[illegible]/Tou[illegible]
LPINDI;
Visas AM 15
ORT THAILAND
STAY 15 DAYS
LEAVE THE
LATER THAN
ATION OFFICER
8 JUN
ADMITT
SAN FRANCISCO
ADM
Visas
MAY 2
17.6.22
DATE
PASSPORT & VISA EXAMINATION
TAIPEI INTERNATIONAL AIRPORT
REPUBLIC OF CHINA
INSPECTOR
TO
IS
within six mo
od of stay: ONE
trips ONE
of journey
issue 2
ollected: Drachmes
THE CO
IMMIGRATION
BAR KED
CEYLON
Consular
1969
VISA
AIRPORT
APR 1973
2074
DIVISION
REGISTR
IMMIGRATION OFFICER

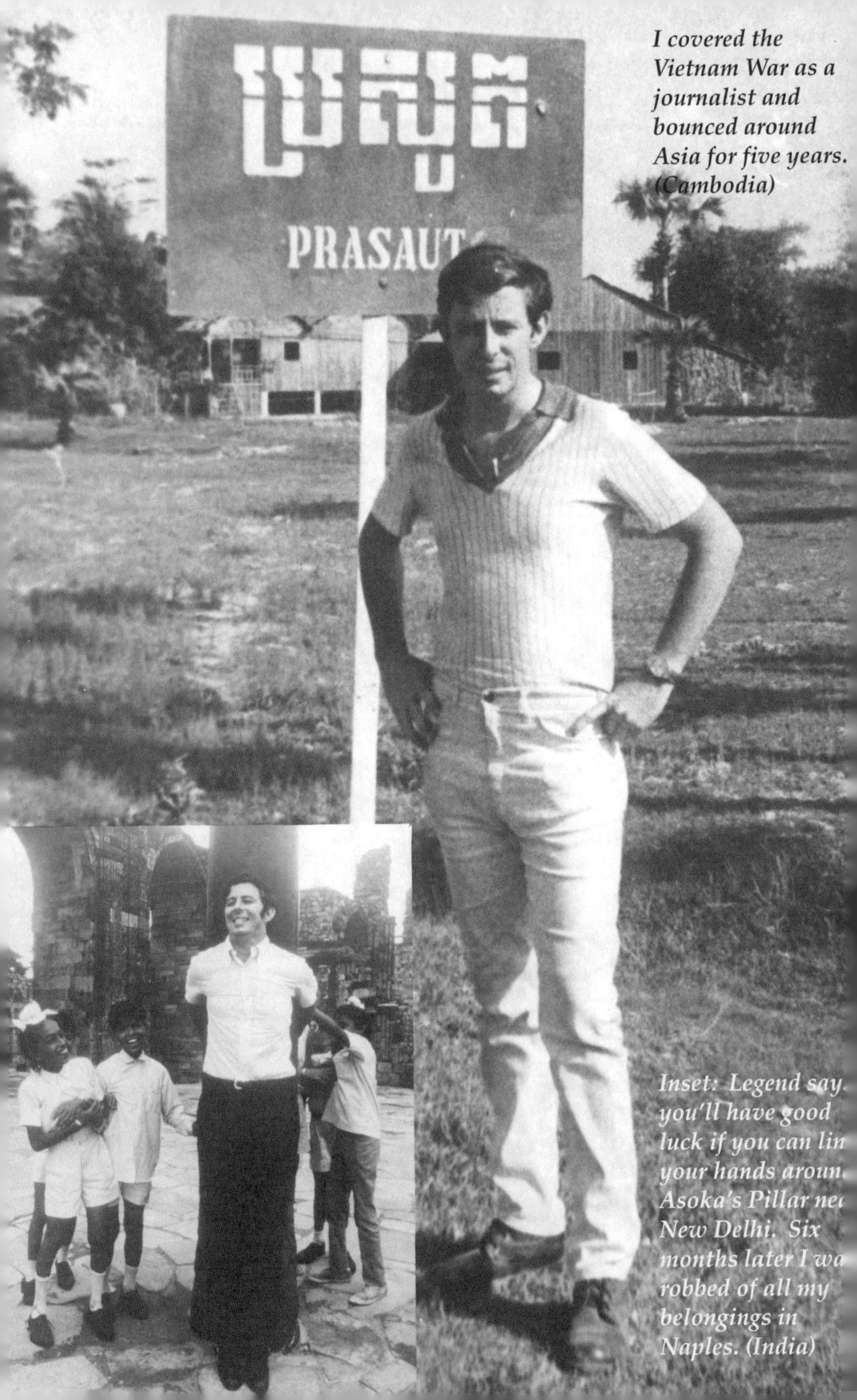

I covered the Vietnam War as a journalist and bounced around Asia for five years. (Cambodia)

Inset: Legend say you'll have good luck if you can lin your hands aroun Asoka's Pillar ne New Delhi. Six months later I wa robbed of all my belongings in Naples. (India)

AT THE AIRPORT

First, which airport?

Do not assume there is only one airport in the city you are visiting. Check before leaving.

Paris has two international airports—Orly and Charles de Gaulle. London has three—Heathrow, Gatwick, and Stansted. Do you know the precise name of the airport where you will be landing and taking off?

And at which terminal. *What?*

Yes, which terminal. This can be crucial information when you are leaving. Paris's Charles de Gaulle has *six* terminals if you include the charter terminal.

I recently passed two highly perturbed Americans at Orly and overheard their conversation. They had taken the bus from Paris to the airport and hadn't realized that the bus stopped at several terminals. The one they chose was the wrong one for their flight. So they were scrambling with their bags to get to the right terminal. Late.

Which airline flies from which terminal is generally marked on the road leading to the airport. A taxi driver will usually drop you off at the right terminal if you give him the name of your airline. I say "usually" because many taxi drivers seem to need a little help these days.

The Best Way

Print the name of your airline, the flight number, and the name of the terminal (e.g., Terminal C) if there is more than one terminal at your particular airport. Show the paper to your driver. If it's a bus driver, ask at which stop to get off—first, second, etc.—and count carefully, looking out the window to spot the name of the your airline. If you aren't sure, ask him again.

Know Your Transit Airport

If you are flying to one airport and changing planes to fly to your final destination, you should know what to expect at your transit airport. Europe has five major transit airports: London's Heathrow, Paris's Charles de Gaulle and Orly, Frankfurt in Germany, and Amsterdam's Schiphol.

When you change planes at Heathrow in England you might find you must take a bus to another terminal, even though you're using the same airline. Heathrow is the worst of the lot. Schiphol in Holland, the smallest of the transit stops, is also the most convenient. If you have a choice make your change there. If you don't, ask your travel agent for details about the airport where you will be changing.

Advance knowledge of what you'll be up against will help keep the stomach from churning and the stress level down, as you strain to hear the barely comprehensible instructions for "transiting passengers" over the address system.

THROUGH THE LOOKING GLASS

You have arrived at the airport. How do you get to the check-in counter? Can you handle your own luggage? Or do you need help?

Sometimes you can find a free baggage cart at the departure entrance. But many airports provide cart service only at the arrival gate. At the departure entrance you're liable to find only porters who expect a tip for moving your bags to the check-in counter.

If you need help, prepare your tip in advance. Ask a local before you leave for the airport how much to tip per bag. In the U.S. a buck a bag is common.

Early Check-In?

Some airports offer a curbside check-in for luggage. A uniformed porter has a stand outside the door leading to the check-in counter for your flight. You show him your ticket and he'll check your bags and give you a baggage claim ticket. A tip is usually in order. Then you move inside to the counter for your passport-and-ticket check-in.

The early check-in is convenient. I've used it. But not without a twinge of uneasiness as to whether my bags would actually wind up on my flight. There's a general feeling—maybe just superstition—that more bags get lost by curbside check-in than otherwise. If you feel too uneasy you can always check your bags at the official check-in counter inside. In either case it pays to know something about the baggage check procedure.

Three Important Letters

LAX has entered the vocabulary of people who travel a lot. LAX is the three-letter symbol for the Los Angeles airport. People speak of flying to LAX, not to L.A.

Every major airport in the world has a three-letter symbol. And that symbol will appear on the baggage tag that the airline employee puts on your bags. You should know the symbol of your airport of arrival. If you are changing flights en route to your final destination, your three-letter symbol will be at the top of the baggage check.

This happened to me recently. It was a domestic flight. I used the curbside check-in. It didn't bother me that the check-in guy, a newly arrived immigrant, barely spoke English. I could speak his language. What bothered me was that he appeared never to have heard of the state where I was headed. And the name of my airport sounded very much like the name of a country in Central America.

Luckily, I had made a point of memorizing the three-letter code for my destination. When I saw him slap the correct baggage routing ticket on my bags, I breathed a great sigh of relief—and over-tipped him.

Ask your travel agent to find the three-letter code for your final destination airport. Not all of them are as obvious as LAX. New York's Kennedy is easy too—JFK. But who would guess, for example, that the code for Washington Dulles International is IAD?

Knowing your baggage code is another small step in the stress management program.

SITTING SMART

Reserve your seat *before* you arrive at the airport. That's the first rule of sitting smart. It's not always possible, I admit, especially if you are sitting in the coach section. Many airlines will book a seat only when you appear at the airport. And all airlines reserve at least some seats for airport check-in only. Which is another reason for showing up early.

If a pre-booking service is available the best way to get a seat reservation is to have your travel agent make it. Depending on the airline and the flight, some travel agents are able to book your seat and even give you a boarding pass when you buy your ticket. If they can't do it then, ask them to do it by telephone later—but as far in advance of your departure as possible.

If you are in a foreign city and not operating with a travel agent, it pays to visit the airline office shortly after you arrive to confirm your return reservation and to book your seat. This will seem a minor inconvenience later when you get to the airport and realize that the plane is full but your chosen seat is waiting for you.

Flying Smart

Where to Sit?

I ask for an aisle seat, on the left-hand side, in the no-smoking section. (When you say left-hand side or right-hand side, add "facing the cockpit from inside," so the reservation agent will know exactly what side you are referring to.)

Why Do I Sit There?

Probably out of some vague superstition. I sat on the left side of airplanes and helicopters during the Vietnam War, and I came out of that disaster okay. I don't like a window seat because I'm a little claustrophobic and hate to be pinned in.

However the window seat offers—besides the view—a more stable position for sleeping. And on the aisle seat you always have to put up with toilet-bound people bumping by, or the food and drink cart threatening to amputate any stray feet.

Aisle or window, left or right side, is a matter of your preference. But you should think in these terms because you don't want to wind up in the middle section on a packed flight. I'll explain.

On an international flight you are likely to be on an airplane configured similar to this:

On the left side, facing the cockpit, are two or three seats. Then a narrow aisle. In the middle are four or five seats, often smaller and with less leg-room. Then another narrow aisle. And on the right side, facing the cockpit, are two or three more seats—aisle and window.

If you are traveling with someone it's better to book the aisle and window seat, no matter if there are three seats in the row. If the plane is crowded and someone has been placed in the middle seat, the person will let you give up the aisle or window so you can sit together.

In fact when you are traveling with someone you have all the more reason to reserve your seat in advance, or to show up at the airport early if you can't. I've seen starry-eyed lovers who waited until they arrived late at the airport to book their seats, only to find themselves separated by half a plane because no two adjoining seats were left. Sometimes people will cooperate and change seats so you can be with your companion. But on packed flights they frequently don't want to bother.

The seats by the emergency exits or next to a bulkhead have the most leg-room, and you can request to be assigned there. (Note: Bulkhead seats are usually airport check-in only.) Sometimes you can't lift up the seat arms to stretch out, though, because they contain the food tables. If you sit closer to the front you can disembark more quickly after landing. But this is a minor convenience because, probably, you will be held up at immigration or customs anyway.

As to which seats are safest in the event of an accident, there are a number of theories. Some suggest that seats in the first third of the plane have a higher survival rate. But there's no sure thing in flying, and I find it best not to dwell on the point.

The Second Rule of Sitting Smart

Your seat is the one that doesn't belong to anyone else.

At the check-in counter I start my campaign to find out in advance if the airplane is full. I'll say to the ticket agent once I'm checked in, "Is the flight crowded?" Usually I get a response. If I don't, it is the first thing I ask the nearest flight attendant when I board.

I'm trying to find out because I want to know whether I can grab two or more seats, to be more comfortable. If it's a crowded flight I know there is little chance. I'll simply have to sit in the seat that has been assigned me. But if I discover it's not a heavy flight I'll immediately start looking around for the best available seats that are not occupied.

What I'm doing is taking advantage of the fact that most passengers don't realize—at least don't realize at first—that you can move around to find a more comfortable situation. You don't have to sit in the seat assigned you if the plane is not full. For weight distribution reasons, the airlines do sometimes require that you stay in your assigned seat until after takeoff.

Of course there's some etiquette involved here. If other people have won the seat assignment lottery and are sitting beside two empty seats, you don't plop down beside them. They get to stretch out. Maybe you'll have the luck next time.

Essentially, choosing a more comfortable location is a matter of first come, first served. I'll tell you more about the Law of the Clouds later.

CHECKING IN

At the airport you are confronted by a multitude of check-in counters. In fact your own airline might be checking passengers for a number of flights at the same time. Or as sometimes happens, you might be checked in by an assisting airline—not the one you'll be flying on. So you've got to recognize more than just the logo of your carrier.

Know Your Flight Number

You know where you are going, and your airline. But to quickly find your check-in counter, you should also know your flight number. The display panel behind your counter will read Uranus Airlines, Flight 079, London. One counter may book only first-class passengers, several others coach class. Another counter may be set aside for unticketed passengers. Make sure you are in the right line.

A Shopping Mall from Hell

Have you ever been in a shopping mall with a waterfall, a piano playing? The idea is to relax you, to take away the tension, to put you in a good mood for shopping. An airport is sort of a shopping mall from hell where everything seems designed to give you more tension, not take it away. In such a pressured atmosphere grown men and women sometimes regress to a childlike state. If they don't exactly forget their names, they tend not to remember the basic information they need to get them on the plane.

As you approach the check-in counter, make sure you have your passport and ticket in hand. Don't hold up the line while you fumble through your purse or bags looking for them. You must give your passport to the agent along with your ticket. The agent will simply verify that the passport is valid and that it bears your photo and name. If you need a visa, that will be checked too, because the airline can be fined if it sends you on without one. Then your passport will be handed back to you.

As you give your ticket and passport to the agent, or even before, place your bags on the scale to the left or right of the counter for weighing. (This is the part where I hold my breath.) If you have bags with shoulder straps, you should have already removed the straps and placed them inside your bags. They might get tangled with other luggage during the loading process. You should have also removed all old airline destination baggage checks from the baggage.

Your conversation with the airline agent should follow along these lines:

"Hello. My final destination is —." *The ticket agent will want to make sure he or she is about to check your bags to your final destination. So volunteer this information immediately.* "I believe I already have a seat reservation." *This helps the agent move faster on the computer. If you don't have a pre-booked seat then say,* "I haven't booked my seat yet. Is it possible to get an aisle (window) seat in the no-smoking section on the left (right) side facing the cockpit?"

If you don't ask for a seat the computer is programmed to assign you one based on the best weight distribution for the plane and the convenience of the passenger—if the two aren't at odds. That is, they aren't supposed to put you in a middle row with three other people if the fight is half empty. But it does happen. And that's another reason why you should take control of your own seat booking.

Also, if you need a wheelchair or need to be boarded early because of an infirmity or because you are accompanying young children, this is the last minute to tell the ticket agent. It's also the last moment to order a special menu (for example, vegetarian) if you are in need. The airlines provide eleven different types of food. Actually, you should have requested a wheelchair or a special meal twenty-four hours in advance.

The agent checks your passport, hands it back, then detaches the flight coupon from your ticket and enters the check-in and seating information in the computer. A key is pressed and out comes your boarding card.

Now we arrive at the ticklish moment when your baggage is tagged. Most bags are never lost. And a bag is seldom really "lost," just misrouted. You file a claim with the airline and they'll have it for you several flights later or the next day.

I've had a number of strays, however. And Claude had her bags lost on three successive flights from Paris to Málaga. If you've memorized your three-letter airport of destination symbol, you will feel a bit of satisfaction when you see the agent stick it on your bags. If you are changing airports en route, your final destination symbol will be at the top. Then you want to make sure that the baggage claim stubs are attached to your ticket envelope.

With that, you are finished at check-in. You have recovered your passport, your ticket, your baggage claim stubs, and your boarding card. The agent has told you at which gate your flight will be boarding and the time—usually twenty or thirty minutes before the flight is scheduled to depart, although on wide-body jets it can be up to fifty minutes.

Now what do you do?

THE WANDERER

I'm not an airport wanderer. Some people are. You can see them walking around with a look of slight confusion, sightseers at the airport. My theory is that you can absorb other people's tensions and anxieties. Then it becomes the monkey on your back. So it's best, I believe, to stay self-focused and move to your boarding gate as quickly as possible.

Moreover, if you are wandering around the airport, you might miss the announcement for your flight. Many airport public address systems leave much to be desired in terms of audio volume and comprehensibility. And some "silent" airports (Stockholm, for example) make no public announcements at all but simply rely on passengers to get their flight information from a display.

You might want to visit a couple of places before you go through security and passport control. First, the duty-free shop. That's where you buy perfume, alcohol, wine, and other luxury items tax free if you are a ticketed international passenger.

At many airports the duty-free shop is located in the area after you go through security and passport control. So you just pay for the goods and take them with you on the spot.

But at other airports (Washington Dulles, for example) the duty-free shop is located in an area that is not limited to international travelers. In this case, you buy your stuff and present your ticket to show you are a genuine international traveler. Your purchase is bagged and sealed and you are given a receipt. An employee from the duty-free shop will be standing at the boarding gate to hand you your purchase after you present your boarding card to the flight agent.

(A flight attendant I know says: *"Passengers should seek information about duty-free prices at a given airport. Prices for the same item may vary enormously from one airport to another. And it's not uncommon to have higher price tags at an airport duty-free shop than at shops in town. Port wines in Lisbon...perfumes in Paris...coffee and gems in Brazil—the list is long."*)

The second thing you should consider doing is to use the airport bathroom if you feel even the slightest urge. If you have young children, don't ask—order. Airport bathrooms are usually clean and spacious, a far cry from the micro-toilet you are going to be using on the airplane.

This is also the time to select your reading material for the flight if you haven't already done so. A newsstand is never far away from the check-in area. If you want to save money, ask the agent at the check-in counter whether reading material is available on the plane. If so, you also want to ask whether it is available for self-service in the boarding lounge, or distributed by the attendants. If it is distributed only, your favorite paper or magazine may be gone before the attendant reaches you.

Once you've done these three things I suggest you head to your boarding gate. And to get there you've got to go through...

SECURITY

Practically everyone these days is familiar with the metal detector—a doorframe-shaped apparatus that buzzes in alarm every time I walk through it with my keys in my pocket. The metal detector is one of three aspects of airport security. The other two are the X-ray device/ conveyer belt and the security agent who is there to handcheck certain items physically—including, sometimes, yourself.

The X-Ray/Conveyer Belt Is First

When you approach security the first thing you do, without being told, is to put all your handbaggage, purses and whatever (with several exceptions I'll mention), on the covered conveyer belt. It contains a device that the security agent uses to visually penetrate and examine what you are carrying aboard the plane. He looks at your stuff on a TV-like monitor. The agent is, of course, looking for weapons or bombs or other dangerous objects.

This is for your protection—and mine. I like to see security agents who are attentive and strict in checking all carry-on items.

Still the X-ray device raises a question as to whether it will damage certain of your belongings. Like film. Or computer diskettes. Some claim it won't; some claim it will.

The way to avoid the issue is not to carry a loaded camera. Put your film, along with your computer diskettes, at the top of one of your carry-ons. Then remove those items before you put the bag on the X-ray/conveyer, and ask the security agent to hand check them.

The Laptop Gambit

More and more people are traveling with laptop computers. And there's still a controversy over whether the X-ray device will mess up the hard drive and the software. I prefer not to take any chances with my machine.

I've had arguments with the security guys about whether I should put my computer through the X-ray/conveyer. And in the process I've learned a little trick that makes it easier to get them to check it by hand.

Before I approach the X-ray/conveyer, I stop and remove my laptop from the computer carrying case. Then I place the carrying case on the conveyer, along with all other handbags, for the required X-ray inspection. As it is underway I call a security agent and give him my computer and ask that it be hand checked.

This is a fait accompli that usually works. You don't want to get into an argument about whether your computer carrying case also should be hand checked. Put it through without saying anything.

The security agent then asks me, after I pass through the metal detector, to open my computer and turn it on to prove it is a working machine. That done, I replace the laptop in its case and recover my other carry-ons.

But let me back up one step, to the metal detector. If you are carrying coins or keys or anything metallic in your pockets, it's better to remove them and put them in the provided plastic bowl next to the detector. Then after you walk through you recover your coins or keys. This saves the inconvenience of your stuff possibly setting off the buzzer, requiring you to repeat the process again after emptying your pockets.

Don't Joke With Security

Take this business seriously. Some people, suffering airport stress, try to make jokes about bombs or weapons as they go through security. Such attempts at humor are not appreciated by the agents or fellow passengers. It could get you in trouble.

Above all, don't try to joke about security matters with the flight attendants once you have boarded. Some people have. And they've suddenly been surrounded and ejected from the plane. Or even arrested.

Airport security is getting tougher—and rightly so. Any items that may present the least danger—a small Swiss army pocket knife, for example—can be taken from you. To get it back after the flight, you give a receipt to a cabin crewmember at the door when leaving, or else to the ground staff in charge of luggage at the baggage carrousel.

BOARDING GATE

When I reach my boarding gate I try to find an end seat close to and facing the gate. An end seat gives you more space to store your carry-ons while you wait. If it is a busy flight you shouldn't take up a second seat with your handbaggage.

Now that I am settled in at the boarding gate I first take a few moments to collect myself. Then I begin to organize for the flight. I place my passport and valuables in a small handbag at the top of the carry-on I intend to stow beneath the seat in front of me. I also check to make sure the several things I'll need during the flight are in that bag and easy to retrieve. From this point, I know that I'll only need my boarding card.

Keep Your Boarding Card Handy

The boarding card looks like a stiff-paper coupon with a detachable stub. It contains the details of your flight, including your seat number, which you should note and remember. You should have it ready to hand to the flight agent when you are called to board. The agent will detach the long part of the boarding card and give you the stub, which contains your seat number.

Flying Smart

To Queue or Not to Queue

Some people start lining up at the gate a few minutes before the boarding time they were given at the check-in counter. Of course, as we know, everybody has been assigned a seat. And indeed the flight agent will probably announce the sequence in which the passengers are to board. For example, the agent might say, "Passengers in rows 32 to 70 will board first."

So what's the rush?

Most people get in line early, I think, out of a sheep-like reaction. I don't bother to stand and wait if the flight is not crowded. Because I know that the real boarding time is most always later than the boarding time announced by the agent at the check-in counter. The pilots can make up for a few minutes of lost time during the flight if the tailwinds are right. And other flights are simply, inexplicably (at least to the passenger), late.

There are, however, a couple of advantages to being the first on the plane in your group if the flight is crowded. You can get to your seat and stow your carry-ons without being blocked by other passengers in the aisle. And it gives you a chance to get an early feel for the plane and to assess the possibility of finding a more comfortable situation.

Generally, I settle down at the boarding gate and begin to read something light. I try not to look at my watch. And I restrain my temptation to question the flight agents when the official boarding time passes and no announcement is made. We're going to be running a little late. But I expected that.

BOARDING

You have presented your boarding card. The agent has returned the stub that has your seat number. Hold the stub as you enter the airplane. A flight attendant will be there to glance at it and point you in the direction of your seat.

Seat assignments carry a number, which is your row, and a letter, which is your actual seat in that row. The seat letters run alphabetically from left to right, and go all the way across the plane. *I* (eye) is usually left out because it is too easily confused for *one*.

Let's say your seat is 38C. You find row 38. You see three seats and the letters above them are marked ABC. The first letter represents the window seat. Therefore you are assigned to the aisle seat.

Boarding is one of the more unpleasant moments of a flight. It's usually full of confusion and bumps. Some people can't find their seats. Others block the aisle while they try to decide where they are going to stow their handbags.

Until you are ready to stow your stuff you should stand

between two rows of seats directly underneath the bin you'll use and let the other passengers pass by in the aisle.

(A flight attendant I know says: *"One thing that turns us cabin crewmembers ugly is when one person stops the whole boarding process by blocking the aisle with a collapsible cart. He or she insists on rolling the baggage in the aisle. It won't fit, of course, and has to be undone inside the plane. Please step aside before you reach the plane door and undo the things on your cart and carry them in by hand."*)

Know in Advance

I already know when I get on the plane where I am going to stow my bags. The one with my valuables and things I'll need on the flight goes under the seat in front. My computer or whatever goes in the storage bin above my head.

You should know too.

It's convenient but not necessary to put your carry-on in the storage bin directly over your row. If the bin is full, find one farther down the line.

Now is also the time to shed your coat and put it in the bin. Don't lay your coat flat the whole length. Fold it neatly and place it on the heavier items in the bin. Usually the plane will be well heated, and you will be issued a small blanket in case you get chilly. Sometimes, though, the plane is not heating well and no blankets are available. To make your own temperature control, wear a lightweight sweater that you can put on or remove and leave in your seat.

You will find, as I've said, that there's really not much space under those seats. So let me repeat my warning.

Your carry-on must conform to size regulations and must be stowed under the seat in front for safety reasons. Carrying a clothes bag is an iffy proposition, and I don't recommend it. But wide-body jets usually have closets to hang clothes, even in coach class. Leave no valuables there.

ANIMAL FRIENDS

No, I am not talking about those sloppy eaters we all know. I'm referring to your pets. Cats and dogs are easy to fly. You must tell the airline in advance, though, when you make your reservation. If you have an animal of less than five kilos (11 pounds), you can carry it with you into the compartment, as long as it is enclosed in a bag or a similar carrier. There's a charge, depending on the current rate. Right now, to fly a dog or cat with you from Paris to New York costs ninety dollars.

Actually it often costs less when you fly a bigger dog, as is required, in the special compartment—which is not, as many people think, the baggage compartment. It is a separate, pressurized compartment that is comfortable for the animal and even quieter than the passenger cabin. Indeed the airlines are very careful with animals. They don't want somebody suing them for an accident, with all the attendant bad publicity that would bring.

When you check in the agent will give you a chit that serves as your pet's ticket. You pay at the counter as you would for excess baggage. If you are boarding a dog bigger than five kilos you must have a carrier. You can rent one from the airline (check to make sure one is available), or bring your own. The dog will be taken from you at the last moment and put in the special compartment. On arrival an airline employee will be at your flight's baggage carrousel with your pet. Sometimes passengers are directed to a special holding room to make the pick up.

Here are some important checkpoints:

Quarantine - You should check to find out if your country of destination has a quarantine or simply doesn't allow your type of pet to enter the country. Call the country's consulate in the U.S. for this info. You can't take a dog to England or Australia, for example. (Technically, you can to England but you would have to leave the animal in quarantine for months.) Other countries have their own rules.

Health Certificate - This is different from your ordinary vaccination papers for your pet. You must have the stamp of a state veterinarian if you are leaving from America. Therefore it's best to start at least a week or more before departure. You can take your pet to your regular vet, who will send the health certificate to a state vet for stamping.

Vaccine - Call the country's consul to make sure you have all the vaccines required for your pet. A rabies shot is generally the only thing required. But make sure it is valid for the length of time you plan to stay.

Prepare Your Pet - If you have a dog give it a good walk before leaving for the airport. Write the pet's name on the top and side of the carrier. If you think your animal needs a tranquillizer for the trip, consult your vet.

There's a limit on how many animals may be taken into the passenger cabin. So reserve early. The plane's captain has a discretionary power over which animals he will allow aboard. On one flight the pilot decided he didn't want a boa constrictor in the cabin even if it weighed less than five kilos.

We have a dog and cat, and we've never had any trouble. Claude found our cat as a stray kitten on the Greek island of Milos. On the trip to Paris the flight attendants paid the kitty more attention than they did the passengers.

CHILDREN SMART

So you are a single parent traveling with two young children, and suddenly you develop a feeling that the other passengers are trying to avoid you. You are not suffering from incipient paranoia. It's true.

Part of the child-avoidance syndrome is based on the God-given nature of things. If an adult finds flying stressful and uncomfortable, then we can safely predict that a child will find it triply so.

But part of the problem, too, is that many parents don't sit down and think through how they are going to occupy themselves during a long flight—much less their children. Result: You'll get dirty looks and feel the exasperation of the other passengers when your children start doing what they normally do every day—that is, act like kids. But flying, as I've said before, is not a normal situation and children need a bit of different attention here.

Board Early

If your children are young the airline will let you board before the other passengers. Even if they aren't so young but you think you may have trouble getting them settled in, check with the flight agent and explain the problem.

Flying Smart

Go for the Middle Row

Some international flights have only two seats on the left and right hand sides. You don't want to be separated from your children (I've seen it happen—a disaster for parents and passengers), so it's best to ask for seats in the middle row, putting yourself in the end seat. With any luck, the rest of the row may be left vacant and the kids can spread out.

Mom in the Middle at Dinner

The flight attendants divide up the seats when they serve, so your children may receive their trays from both aisles—out of your reach. A mother or a father can avoid the confusion that usually ensues by placing her or himself between the children at mealtimes.

Game the Kids to Sleep

This is not the time for games that beep or squeak and disturb other passengers. But anything else goes, in your campaign to occupy and distract the children until they fall asleep.

Baby Stuff

If your child is under age two, you will be charged generally at a rate of ten percent of a normal ticket. But your baby doesn't get a seat. You must hold the baby on your lap or in a hammock. If you hit the right airline the flight attendants will provide you with a cradle that can be installed over the seat. Baby meals will be provided if you ask in advance. But call 24 hours before departure, because sometimes the baby food is not stocked on the plane. If you are flying smart you will carry your own baby meal and avoid relying on the airline. If your child is over two but under ten, the airlines normally charge fifty percent of the fare—and the kid gets a seat.

Check all this information out, though, when you make your reservation. Rules and regulations vary from country to country.

Unaccompanied Minors

The airlines are used to dealing with unaccompanied minors. They understand your anxiety about sending a child on a flight alone. Your absolute and inviolate duty is to insure that your child is met and picked up at the other end by a reliable friend or relative. If nobody is there for the pick-up when the flight arrives, the airline will not turn over your child to an adult passenger who may volunteer to help. You must provide the airline with the name and telephone number of the friend or relative, in case the specified adult is not there to meet your child.

WHEELING IT

This is a story my mother still tells, ten years later, in her how-I-barely-escaped-disaster voice:

She had a heart condition and needed a wheelchair to travel. That was no problem. The airlines provide wheelchairs. But they expect you to handle your own arrangements after you arrive. So Claude and I were supposed to be there to take over. But we weren't. We were at the wrong gate.

An airline employee started wheeling my mother toward the taxi line, after he picked up her baggage. He couldn't speak English; she couldn't speak French. Here she was headed to a taxi whose driver couldn't speak English either! And she hadn't even written down my address or phone number.

I don't think she was ever happier to see me than at that moment when I intercepted her, as the airline guy, speaking reassuringly in French, was about to wheel her out the airport exit.

The point, of course, is this: Departing from the States in a wheelchair is no problem—but make sure you have your arrangements on the other end worked out carefully in advance.

The airlines are ready to deal with anything from serious stretcher cases to people who merely need help walking up stairways. In the case of a life-threatening incapacitation, the passenger's doctor should phone the airline's medical department and work out the details. This has to be done 48 to 24 hours in advance, because the airline must agree to take the passenger.

More typically, people who need help fall into two categories: The ambulatory (like my mother) who need the helping hand of another person or a wheelchair ride; and those who are completely wheelchair bound.

If you are in a wheelchair you should let the airline know 24 hours in advance, although they aren't going to faint if you show up unannounced through no fault of your own. Get there early.

Chances are, your wheelchair is too small to work in the plane. So they'll take your chair, store it in a compartment, and transfer you to an airline wheelchair. You will be preboarded before the other passengers. On arrival you will be the last to leave the plane. Your wheelchair will be reassembled and waiting for you in the baggage area. Once you are transferred back to your own chair the airline relinquishes responsibility.

Now that's the way it works—in theory. What sometimes happens in reality is that you spend more time than you'd like waiting for a chair on arrival. This is because international flights usually arrive at the same time and there are only so many wheelchairs available. National—that is, state—airlines usually make sure their passengers are served first.

So a little patience is required for wheeling-it. But I suspect you've already developed that. Also, as I've said, careful prior planning. Some countries—in fact, I'd say most countries—aren't as sensitive to the needs of people wheeling-it as the United States has become in the past few years. Ramps aren't as common and bathrooms are not as well equipped (though you won't have a problem on the plane). But things are changing, especially in Western Europe.

Wheeling-it simply depends on the individual and how easily one deals with the challenges. I have a friend who had a serious stroke, and he flies all over the world without help. He travels with only one suitcase—that's important, go light. And he's an I-can-handle-anything sort of guy.

If you are like him you'll probably get around easier than I do. I have a lousy sense of direction and orientation. I can get lost going from here to the corner.

THEY KNOW YOU

Well, they don't know me. The flight attendants, I'm talking about. Actually, that's not true. They do know me—as an ordinary passenger. They know everybody on the flight, because they have what is called a "Passengers Information List."

The PIL tells them about special cases, such as passengers with medical problems, passengers in wheelchairs, unaccompanied minors, VIPs, passengers with babies or pets, passengers who belong to airline clubs, passengers who have paid to have an extra empty seat. You might need to remind them sometimes. But don't worry, you are listed if you told the airline in advance.

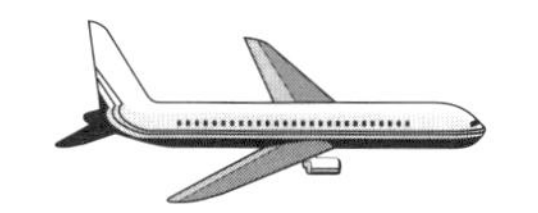

LESS IS LESS

Less is definitely not more when it comes to an airplane seat. But seats seem to shrink with each passing year, as the airlines try to maximize their profits. If the trend continues I suspect we might need a shoe-horn to get seated.

Nevertheless the seat is going to be your home for the next few hours. You must squeeze what comfort you can by knowing how it works.

Seatbelt

Remember the old-fashioned car seatbelts? You inserted the flat piece of metal on the right into the head on the left and heard a satisfying click? If you wanted to adjust the size you fed a little more of the upper strap into the head and pulled?

Well, that's your airplane seatbelt today.

I don't strap in when I first get on the plane. I might have to stand to let somebody get to the seats next to me. Or I might be asked to help someone store a heavy carry-on in an upper bin. But once the flight is ready to depart, I fasten my seatbelt and don't unstrap again until after landing, except for trips to the lavatory.

The pilot gives you the option of unfastening your seatbelt after he has reached his cruising altitude. The seatbelt sign up ahead (next to the no-smoking sign) will be turned off. If the crew anticipates turbulence you will be told to re-fasten your seatbelt and the sign will light up again.

I'm always surprised when most of the passengers immediately unfasten their seatbelts when they are given the permission. Remember: It's an option, not a command. You can remain just as comfortable and still be protected if you loosen your seatbelt a bit instead of taking it off.

Do I sound overly cautious? You see, I've been on several flights when we hit an unexpected air pocket—known as "clear-air turbulence"—and suddenly dropped like a rock for a few thousand feet. No one was hurt on my flights. But I know of people who have been injured when they weren't belted up and the same thing happened. It's not likely to happen to you...but...

Figuring Out the Buttons

On your armrest to the left you'll see various buttons and a jack plug-in. I still get a little confused on some flights deciding which is what. The easiest one is the little sketch of a lightbulb. That's the on/off switch for your overhead light. Another has a pictogram of a woman. That's to call the flight attendant. Then you've got the numbered channels for music and the movie next to the plug-in jack for your headphones. Technology is changing so fast that many planes now have small TV sets for each seat.

Somewhere on the left armrest, in front or on the side, is a larger button you can push to make the seat recline. Since the seat must remain in the upright position for takeoff, you shouldn't recline it when you first get on the plane.

A small table is folded into the seat in front of you. You let it down by flipping the latch at the top. Below the table is a cloth pocket that contains an inflight magazine and a plastic card showing the configuration of the airplane you are on. The first section of the magazine provides a lot of information about what you need to know to be comfortable.

Pinpoint Your Position

You should take a look at the configuration card and fix your location in terms of the nearest emergency exit and lavatory. Then you should carefully study your immediate area to make sure you can find your way back to your seat in the dark. Don't depend simply on the dimly lit seat numbers above your row.

I once returned from the lavatory and found a woman sitting in my place. It was a good seat, and I told her that I preferred to keep it. She said, sorry, it was her seat. I tried to persuade her to move, growing increasingly angry. Finally, she suggested that I look at the seat number on my boarding card stub.

What a red face! And this happened in broad daylight. All because I had not taken the time to properly orient myself. Look to your left, right, in front and behind. Note the characteristics of the people around you (the guy's bald, the woman's blonde) so you can pinpoint your position.

The Takeoff Wait

Once you are settled in your seat you are ready for takeoff. Unfortunately the flight crew is not. Minutes pass and you are told nothing. I find the takeoff wait a little irritating even though I realize the delay is probably beyond the pilot's control.

When the pilot leaves the parking area he falls under the jurisdiction of the airport's Air Traffic Control. ATC gives him taxi clearance and assigns a runway. If it's a busy time when lots of flights are leaving he may have to wait a while for a runway assignment. The reason the crew doesn't tell the passengers what is going on is because they often don't know themselves. Or they receive new or contradictory orders.

The first and most important sign that takeoff is imminent comes when you see the flight attendants checking the emergency exit doors. You might hear them say, "Armed and cross-checked." This is a required procedure. They are putting the escape and evacuation slides in the "on" position.

Which means that if you pull the emergency handle the door will open and the escape slide will deploy. This can't happen while the plane is in the air. Pressurization prevents the door from coming open whether the handle is turned or not.

A YOUNG OLD PLANE

Now that you are in effect trapped in your seat it's time for a little pep talk. Statistics prove that flying is less dangerous than driving a car to the local shopping mall. In fact many more air crew members get killed on the way to the airport than on airplanes. And airplanes don't get old very fast. They are checked and rechecked after every flight. The engine is overhauled every five thousand flight hours. Parts are usually replaced, not repaired.

For every important system in a plane there's a backup system. Sometimes two. Four-engine planes are designed to fly with only two engines; two-engines, with one. The flight crew is in constant touch with air traffic controllers on the ground and other planes in the air. Every aspect of safety has been tested to meet any kind of contingency.

Then why are we so aware of airplane crashes?

They make the news. Auto wrecks seldom do. Think of the thousands of flights every day without a single incident. Remember that all the cockpit-crew members are pilots. The captain is not just a pilot who has been casually assigned. He is specifically qualified to fly your aircraft, and he's probably made this same flight dozens of times.

Zalin Grant

All things considered, flying is the safest transport system ever devised by man.

Have I convinced you?

I doubt it. I haven't even convinced myself. But I know the facts don't lie: You and I have nothing to worry about on this flight. Fear is natural. But we shouldn't let it rise to the level of the irrational. To help keep it in check, I'll tell you about several things that rattled me on my early flights.

BUMP BUMP AND AWAY

Even before we started moving I was disturbed to feel the plane shuddering spasmodically and to hear what sounded like somebody thumping on its underside. It turned out they were just loading the luggage in the baggage compartment. *(What? My suitcase!)* The thumping sound gives you a feeling that the plane is really flimsy, but it's not.

Then when we started taxiing down the runway I thought I was riding on a tractor instead of a multi-million dollar airplane. Bumpety-bump. It was not a smooth ride. I was surprised. And the pilot was putting on his brakes and releasing them and then doing it again like a novice driver—or someone drunk. Did he know what he was doing?

Yep, he did. The bumpy ride to the runway came from the fact that nearly fifty thousand pounds of weight was riding on each landing gear wheel. The braking was necessary in the same way that you must brake your car and then release when it is idling at a high speed and moving. The pilot brakes until the plane is traveling slowly, then releases until it reaccelerates, and repeats the procedure to slow it down again.

I was happy to take off before the bumpy ride convinced me I was on a broken-down plane. So when I heard the engines revving mightily and felt the huge thing moving down the runway faster and faster and finally lifting off quite smoothly, I felt a flutter in my stomach but also a sense of relief.

But damn! Suddenly I felt the plane shudder and heard a loud mechanical sound that scared the sweat out of me. Were we going down? Nope. The pilot was just retracting the landing gear, which folded into its housing under the plane. It makes a lot of noise, so just ignore it.

The nose was up and we were climbing at an angle of about fifteen degrees. My ears started popping. The climb seemed to go on forever. Actually it took between six and ten minutes. Then the pilot reached his cruising altitude which was around 35,000 feet and leveled off.

I began to feel better. But I wondered why the pilot and crew had not told me about the things that had worried me—the bumpy ride, the landing gear retraction. Later I found out that the FAA prohibits the crew from talking to the passengers from the time the aircraft is moving until it reaches ten thousand feet, unless there's something directly related to a safety matter. This frees the crew to focus their concentration on taking off.

PRESIDENTIAL SMART

The first time I flew on Air Force One with the President of the United States I was with four other journalists. We had been picked by the press secretary as "pool" reporters to have dinner with Lyndon Johnson and to cover his return to Washington. The rest of the White House press corps followed us in a chartered jet.

Lyndon Johnson was bigger than life and always full of surprises. But I was frankly shocked by the first thing he did when he sat down with us after Air Force One reached its cruising altitude. He took off his tie, unbuttoned his shirt, and called for an air force steward. The young enlisted guy arrived and immediately dropped to his knees in front of LBJ.

"Geez!" I thought. "Is he going to kiss the President's feet?"

Then I saw that he was removing LBJ's shoes and replacing them with bedroom slippers.

I was so amazed by the imperial way Johnson was conducting himself that at first I didn't consider what he was doing. But later when I thought about it, it made sense.

LBJ may have had a swollen head but he wasn't going to have swollen ankles. The Prez was flying smart.

Body fluids collect in the lower extremities during a long flight. This swells up the feet and ankles and sometimes the lower legs. The discomfort can be significant.

So I always pull an LBJ as soon as the plane lifts off. I must admit, though, that no one has ever dropped to their knees and removed my shoes. I do it myself and replace them with the airline slippers that I've collected from first-class cabins over the years.

If you don't have sock slippers, I suggest you carry a pair of larger comfortable clean socks or even lightweight bedroom slippers to put on during the flight. Wear them to the lavatory and then discard them before you land. If taking off your shoes during the flight doesn't appeal to you, you might consider at least unlacing or unstrapping your footwear.

Better still, flying stockings are now available on the market. They evolved from the old anti-varicose vein stockings but look much better. You'll notice that many female flight attendants wear them. They keep the blood flowing freely in your legs. The same type in men's socks is also available.

For the guys this is the time to unbuckle your belt and unzip a little. You can do this discreetly by using the small blanket you have been issued as a cover for that area. Believe me, you'll feel better at the end of the flight.

But back to my LBJ story:

I had planned to use this relatively intimate dinner with LBJ on Air Force One, which took place in December 1967, to submit my opinion that he should close down the Vietnam War as soon as possible. I would do it cautiously, of course, since I knew that I stood in the ranks of what he called "piss-ant reporters." The most mellow moment to make my pitch, I believed, would be after the air force stewards finished serving our desserts.

While screwing up my courage, I noticed that Johnson, who was sitting to my left, was eyeing my apple pie, as he wolfed down his dietary Jell-O.

"Lady Bird wants me to stick to my diet," the President confided to me.

Then he suddenly leaned over, thrust his elbow hard into my chest, and quickly spooned all my pie into his mouth.

So much for my attempt to end the Vietnam War.

DON'T DRINK AND FLY

Lyndon Johnson was known to take a drink. In fact, he would pour his favorite scotch into a bourbon bottle so he would look more like a good ol' boy and not so hoity-toity. But I noticed he did not drink alcohol during our flight. Again, the Prez was flying smart.

Drinking alcohol may not be too smart in any case. But drinking on a long flight is clearly dumb. Alcohol does all the wrong things to your body. To begin with, it reinforces jet lag and makes it difficult for you to adjust to a new time zone. You can get rid of a hangover relatively easy. But jet lag can linger on and on and ruin your trip.

Of course a glass of wine or a beer with dinner is not likely to bother you. But the kind of toss'em-backs people often do on domestic flights will cost you in the end on an international flight.

As for smoking, I'm not even going to get into that. I think you know.

BUT DON'T DRY OUT

You are going to be hit with dehydration on a long flight. Dryness of the skin, throat, mouth and nose. It comes from a lack of humidity in the plane's recirculated air. Which causes you to lose excessive amounts of fluid when you breathe or perspire.

Why can't the carrier keep the proper amount of moisture in the air? It's a matter of cost. The airlines consider it impractical to carry the weight of water that would be needed to maintain the humidity at the same level as in your home or office.

So it's up to you to keep from drying out.

A Half-Bottle of Water

My prime anti-dehydration fighter is a half-bottle of water. I use Evian only because it is widely sold in the U.S. Matter of fact that's not the kind I drink when I'm in France. Any water you normally drink works fine, even the tap water from your home.

But you should have at least a half-bottle stowed in easy reach in your carry-on. I recommend a half-bottle simply because of weight considerations. I take a sip or two every hour or so to counter my fluid loss. That's my rhythm. But you'll find yours.

Why Not Juice, Soft Drinks, or Coffee?

Juice, sure. It's a good replacement fluid, up to a point. Drinking an excessive amount of juice, however, can upset your digestive system, and we're trying hard to guard that like a jewel. Soft drinks are not bad except for putting sugar and chemicals in your body that will contribute to jet lag.

Coffee and tea, being diuretics, stimulate urine production and make you lose even more fluid. Alcohol does too. Which is another reason why drinking and flying is dumb.

All things considered, that simple and wonderful stuff called water works best to combat drying out.

Candy and Tears

I also pack some mints to help keep my mouth and throat from drying out. And artificial tears. The lack of humidity is especially hard on your eyes. If you wear contact lens, I suggest you remove them before the flight and go back to glasses.

I also carry a small spray can of French mineral water—Vittel or Evian. This might be a little too exotic for your tastes. But giving your face a short spray of pressurized water every several hours keeps your skin from drying out.

Moisturizing cream, every woman's friend, will work as well. Men shouldn't resist the idea of carrying a small tube of the stuff to use during the flight. In fact, guys, ask your wife or companion for a recommendation. You might wind up using it after the flight.

And of course mouth spray. It's hardly the height of propriety to spray your breath in public. But all the negative factors hammering away at your body on an airplane create a special situation. Bad breath is a given. Quickly and discreetly, take care of the problem.

Zalin Grant

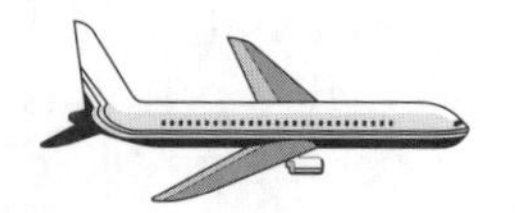

THE LAW OF THE CLOUDS

I told you I would say more about the Law of the Clouds after you got aboard the plane. If you have an aisle or window seat next to two unoccupied seats, you are okay. That's enough stretch-out room. But if someone is next to you or only a seat away, you should focus your attention on the four-or-five seat middle row.

If you see an empty middle row, quickly move into the *second* seat. No one is likely to sit down on either side of you, and possibly the fourth seat will be left vacant too. Loosen your seat belt so you can turn and recline. Then lift up the seat arms.

Voilà! You now have a makeshift bed. Of course it's not a very comfortable bed. The armrests don't raise all the way and there is always some kind of metal trying to bite into your back. But it's as good as you are going to get.

The technique you must use to get the best seats reminds me of the time I hopped a U.S. Marine C-130 to Da Nang. I was with a friend, Associated Press photographer Rick Merron. The rest of the group waiting to board the plane consisted of a hundred tough American marines—and four French nuns.

Flying Smart

"Let's test your mettle, Grant," Rick the photographer laughed. "We'll see if you're really a hardcore war correspondent, or just a Saigon safari suit. There are only eight canvas seats on the plane. Everybody else will have to sit jammed on the floor.

"Are you ready to fight your way through the marines and push the nuns out of the way to get a seat?"

I didn't get the chance. The French nuns were all elbows when the door opened. They cut through the marines like butter. We followed close in their black-habited wake, and wound up with two seats next to them.

What I'm saying is that the Law of the Clouds requires a little pushy initiative. As long as you don't disturb the other passengers or take up more than your share the flight attendants will accept your new location without comment. Except, as I've mentioned, when there's a weight distribution problem.

Actually, I'm sort of sorry I told you this. You'll probably beat me to the best seats on my next flight.

FLIGHT ATTENDANTS

Back in the days of yore flight attendants were called stewardesses. ("Stews," by those of us who were stopover acquaintances.) They were young and single, beautiful and bright. And so desirable they made a guy's teeth hurt.

Some of them still are. But things change with time. (Like me: I had no gray back then.) Age discrimination, weight discrimination, marriage discrimination—years of lawsuits have produced a new kind of flight attendant. More guys, for one thing. And I was on a flight recently with an attendant who looked as though she could've been *my* grandmother.

Still, flight attendants often get a bad rap. They are accused of having plastic smiles and being inattentive. You'd wear a plastic smile too if you had to listen to as many inane comments every day as they do. And who wouldn't try to ignore passengers who assume you are their personal maid.

Let's face it, their job is tougher than it looks. Studies have shown that female attendants go through menopause earlier than the general population. And all of them suffer a higher rate of colds and infections. Which is why they are allowed to fly only a certain number of days per month.

Nonetheless the flight attendants are there to help you. The requirement is for one attendant for every fifty seats. If there are 175 seats there must be a minimum of four attendants. Usually there are more because the airline is trying to keep your business.

Principles for Flight Attendant Handling

Be polite, of course. One plastic smile deserves another. Don't try to make passes. They've been there, done that, heard it all. If they are interested, you'll be the first to know. Lame jokes are going to bring on a phony response, so why bother? If drinks have already been served and you want another, it's easier to walk to the galley yourself than to keep buzzing the attendant. Or wait till one passes and flag her down. Save your requests for important things, such as help with your baby's bottle.

I have very little contact with flight attendants.

"Hello."

"Hello, no thank you."

"Are you sure?"

"I'm sure, yes, thank you."

Because I don't dance to their rhythm.

Part Three

This is my favorite photo of Claude. (Spain) Above: I'm a lousy packer, so Claude does my bags—and I find her car keys.

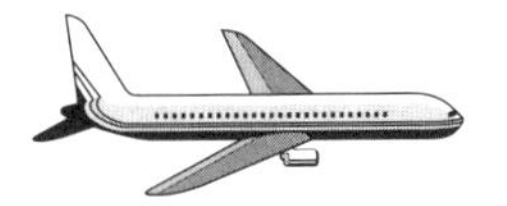

DANCE TO YOUR RHYTHM

The airplane has reached its cruising altitude and the seatbelt sign goes off. An announcement is made that headphones and a menu will be distributed by the attendants, then drinks and dinner will be served.

A feeling of relief, even euphoria, courses through the plane like an electrical charge when the passengers hear this news. Finally, thank God or Buddha or Allah, the airport and boarding chaos is over. Their lives are returning to a semblance of normality, to a predictable schedule.

Dinner Will be Served

It's this craving for a return to normalcy, I believe, that leads many people to flip their tables open in anticipation. They aren't really hungry. But dinner is on the schedule, and it feels reassuring to get back once again to the familiar.

The airlines, of course, are engaging in the psychology of crowd manipulation. They understand perfectly how you feel. They are setting out to lull you into a calmer state, and to control you with a schedule that will work for the convenience of all the passengers and the airline crew too.

You will be served a drink, then dinner. After the trays are cleared away you will be shown a movie. After the movie ends the lights will remain off. Sleep time. An hour or so before the plane begins its landing approach comes a breakfast snack and juice, coffee or tea.

Perhaps all this sounds a bit like your normal evening schedule at home, no?

That's the psychological point.

But wait! You aren't at home. You are sitting in a metal tube high in the sky. It's sort of a low-grade version of the "Back to the Future" time machine we see in movies. You are either losing hours (flying east) or gaining hours (flying west). Either way, your body is growing confused from the abrupt changes in time. Your preparation to enter your new time zone must begin now.

I never eat airline food. My next full meal will be eaten at whatever hour it normally falls in my new time zone. Thus I will try to make it as easy as possible for my digestive system to make the metabolic change to the new time.

The airlines would probably love it if I recommended that you not eat anything on the plane either. But I won't do that. You might be hungry. And, after all, you are paying for it. But I will recommend that you test yourself to see if you are really hungry—or whether you are falling for the psychology of the planned schedule.

If you are not hungry, don't eat. (Airline food isn't very good anyway—surprise!) If you are feeling hungry but not ravenous, eat only the amount that will cut your appetite. If you are on a long flight, try to time your consumption to the eating hours of your final destination—breakfast at the new time zone hour, etc.

The point is that you should dance to your own rhythm—whatever it may be. Our goal is to make your adjustment to the new time zone as smooth as possible, so you can enjoy your trip to the fullest.

Whoa, I'm getting the food cart before the horse. Let's back up to the moment the aircraft reaches its cruising altitude and the seatbelt signs goes off. *Bonggg!*

WHAT TIME IS IT?

We're about to land after a long grueling flight. Someone waves to get the attention of a flight attendant. "What time is it?" the passenger chirps.

"Wow," I'm thinking. "Here's a passenger blissfully riding the jet-lag special. Doesn't have the slightest clue."

I set my watch to my new time zone the moment the plane reaches cruising altitude. That's my first in-flight anti-jet lag action. I recommend that you do the same.

Looking at your watch during the flight, especially if you are losing hours, can be a little depressing after you re-set. Wham! You've just lost six or ten hours of your life. Still, it plays a small but important role in preparing yourself for your new time zone. When you land and step off the plane your mind will not be shocked to see that it's mid-morning or noon, rather than late afternoon or evening as your body continues to believe.

Spring/Forward Fall/Back

You can use the same little trick for remembering how to change your watch for spring and fall to remember the times in Europe and Asia. If you are going overseas, spring forward in time. Coming home to the U.S. you turn back your watch.

Let's say we're looking at the face of a clock with the hands positioned at high noon Eastern Standard Time. Europe is a half clock in front of us—that is, six p.m. Asia is a full clock ahead—midnight. Any country between Europe and Asia falls in between those two times.

Of course I'm talking approximate times as a memory trick. Now let's take some specific times. London is five hours ahead of the U.S. east coast. All the other major cities of Western Europe—Paris, Rome, Berlin, Stockholm, Madrid, Zurich—are six hours ahead. So are Warsaw and Prague. But Moscow is eight hours ahead.

At noon New York time it's already midnight in Bangkok and two a.m. the next morning in Tokyo. In Sidney, Australia, it's three a.m. the next day—meaning 15 hours ahead of us. In New Delhi, India, which is in between New York and Tokyo, it's 10:30 p.m.

The time difference for South America is so little as not to cause much worry. (We're flying south.) Rio is two hours ahead of New York. But it's a long flight.

So you're leaving Paris at eleven a.m. for your home in California. What's your real time? That's right, two a.m. Minus six hours to the east coast, minus three more to the west coast. Re-set your watch soon as you takeoff and let your body begin to readjust to your normal time. Remember: Spring forward when you leave the States, fall back when you return.

This Shop Closes at 19h00

In Europe the twenty-four hour clock system is often used to indicate shop and office hours. This confuses some

Americans. Midnight under this system is 00h00 (the h standing for hours), which means that 6 a.m. is 6h00 and noon is 12h. Easy so far. But what is 5:45 p.m.? That's 17h45.

Naturally, you can continue to count after the noon hour by adding one hour to the next hour (1 p.m. is 13h, 2 p.m. is 14h etc.). But here's a little trick. When the clock reaches one p.m., start adding two to the basic number. You know there's going to be a 1 as the first digit, and beginning with 8 p.m., a 2. So what is 7 p.m.? Add two to the basic number and you get 19h. If 8 p.m. is 20h00, what is 23h00 in our time? Right, you subtract two in this case—11 p.m.

Someone told me they found this trick a little complicated. If you do too, just call 1 p.m. 13h and then 14h—and rock around the rock.

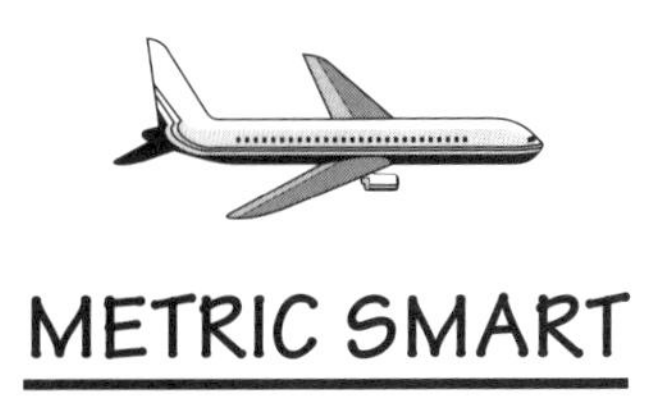

METRIC SMART

Metric smart, I ain't. When I'm in France I still have to ask Claude how tall I am. "Are you sure that's 5'10 in real height?" And don't ask me to figure out the metric area of a square or a cube or anything. I have picked up a couple of everyday survival tricks, though.

How Many Miles Is That?

The sign says fifty kilometers. Just multiply by 6 and knock off the last zero—30 miles. A kilometer is roughly .6 of a mile, so we are actually multiplying the kilometers by six tenths. That's not precisely accurate. But knocking off the last digit after you multiply by six works fine—unless you happen to be employed by NASA.

How Hot Is It?

Boy, this is another one I have to think about. But it works. To convert Celsius (centigrade) to Fahrenheit, multiply by two and add thirty. You see a temperature sign in Europe that says 20 degrees. Two times twenty equals 40 plus thirty equals 70. Now it begins to feel pleasant, like home: 70 degrees F.

WATCH YOUR HEAD

I've advised you to decide, even before you step on the plane, what you are going to put in the overhead bin and what you are going to stow under the seat in front. Unfortunately some passengers will not engage in the same preplanning. They'll stow stuff in the overhead bin and then remember it contains something they need during the flight. So when the seatbelt sign goes off, here they come.

If the bin happens to be located over your head this is the time for you to pay serious attention. The takeoff and climb can disarrange the contents of the compartment. So someone flips open the bin and out falls a heavy brief case. Which breaks the neck of the person seated underneath. It's happened. People have been killed that way. Keep your eyes up any time during the flight and upon landing when someone is fiddling with the storage bin above you.

BATHROOM SMART

The airlines call them lavatories or toilets. Back in the good old days they used to serve as the spur-of-the-moment meeting place for the "Mile-High Club." Couples joined the club by sneaking into the lavatory together and engaging in a delightful, stress-relieving act of the sort that usually took place in the bedroom back home. (Me? Don't ask!) But I haven't heard much talk of the Mile-High Club lately. Probably because airline bathrooms seem to have shrunk (you'd have to be a circus contortionist now), and because flying has become less fun and more mechanistic in form and service.

The number of lavatory/toilets on your plane is based on the assumption that a quarter of the passengers will use the bathroom every hour. The problem with that assumption, I find, is that passengers tend to try to use the toilet within the same ten-minute stretch of certain hours—right after eating, right before landing. This leads to waiting lines and bathrooms that sometimes look like the one I had to share with two dozen other international travelers at a pension in Kabul, Afghanistan. Not exactly a wonderful experience, I might mention.

So being bathroom smart is important to your flight, and I am going to walk you through the numbers.

First, you should pinpoint the nearest lavatory as soon as you are seated. If you can't visually spot it, look at the configuration card in the seat pocket in front of you. Then look for the illuminated lavatory sign to your front or rear. It shows a pictogram of a toilet. A green sign means toilets are available for use. Red means they are all occupied. Watch for the changing colors before you move.

When to Go

I suggested that you use the airport bathroom before boarding. With the effects of airplane dehydration, this should hold you for some time. But one can't really predict the body's response to such upsetting conditions. If you feel the urge after you get on the plane, watch for the seatbelt sign to go off after cruising altitude is reached—and pop out of your seat right then. Be the first.

Lost Sheep

The flight attendants will soon be rolling out a stainless steel cart to serve drinks. The cart takes up the whole aisle. There are always what I call "lost sheep." Passengers who decided to use the bathroom after the attendants started serving drinks. They can't get past the cart to return to their seats, so they have to follow behind, looking a little lost and stupid. This is what you want to avoid. If you've got to go, do it before they roll out the cart.

Between Drinks and Dinner

There is a short period between drinks and dinner when the aisles are free and you can make a bathroom trip. But avoid the time period when the attendants are serving.

There's the cart again, and now they are rushing back and forth bringing more trays or taking them away. As you would expect, after dinner is rush hour at the toilets.

Night Vision

Actually the best time to use the lavatories is after the lights go off and the movie is being shown. People get absorbed by the movie and traffic dies down. This is my time to go, and I always carry a small "Squeeze-it" flashlight in my easy-to-reach carry-on. I use the light to find the lavatories and, most importantly, to find my way back to my seat in the relative darkness.

Before the Breakfast Crunch

A breakfast snack will be served about an hour before the plane lands. Which means you want to brush your teeth, wash up, and make preparations for your return to earth *before* the snack is served. Because the snack routine is a way of waking sleeping passengers. And of course it suddenly hits everyone that a trip to the lavatory is in order. Lines form again.

Open Shut Lock

Airline toilets confuse a lot of people. Some of them still confuse me. First, how do you get in? There's a slot about eye level on the door that says either "Occupied" or "Vacant." If it is vacant, turn the knob and walk in. Except on planes like the one I recently encountered: there, you push the door forward and it folds inward like an accordion and you walk in. Anyway, instructions are written on the door, so that's why it is important to have a little flashlight if you are doing this during dark hours.

Once inside, all toilets are the same. You close the door

and push to the opposite side the lever which is attached to the door at eye level. This locks the door and turns on the light. You press the handle for water on the faucet and it runs automatically for 15 seconds. You don't have much control over these things. There are paper towels and a trash container built into the wall. Don't stuff towels or pads or extraneous items in the toilet.

The toilet flush button is to the side. The first time I pushed a flush button on a plane it made such an incredible noise—*whooosshh!*—that I jumped back in fright. I thought the thing was going to suck me down and out into the sky. The flushing motor operates on four horsepower or more—twice the force of a typical lawnmower. It's a way of using less water, and all wastes are funneled to a holding tank and emptied while on the ground.

For women: I don't have to tell you that men sometimes can be thoughtless beasts. There's a movement on to separate airline toilets into male and female. But right now they are still unisex. If you've developed your own emergency procedures for handling sloppy toilets, now is the time to implement Plan X.

And for everyone: Don't conduct yourself like my fellow travelers in Afghanistan. Think of the person following you to the bathroom. Somebody, somewhere up there, is writing all this down in your personnel file.

WINING AND DINING

Major airlines serve nearly 200,000 free soft drinks every day. Imagine the space that would take up in their planes if every passenger was given a full can. That's why the flight attendant, when you ask for a soft drink, is going to give you only several ounces in a small plastic glass, with a couple of ice cubes.

And it's also why when you ask for a Pepsi you'll likely get Coke or vice versa. An airplane can't carry a wide enough selection to satisfy every customer.

The same attitude carries over to the food. Some airlines do better than others. And you'd think from some of their advertisements that you are about to dine in a three-star restaurant.

Nevertheless, we're talking about mass feeding here. You will usually be given a choice between a meat and a seafood course, both with fancy names. But this is not the moment to entertain thoughts of sending your dish back to the chef. Naturally, if something is demonstrably bad, you should complain. We must keep them on their toes. But airline food is what it is—airline food.

There are a couple of things you can do to make the win-ing and dining experience transpire as smoothly as pos-sible. First, you can get an idea of what drinks are avail-able by looking at the drink cart before it reaches you and by watching what the flight attendants are serving. There's always some bore who will hold up the entire process by demanding a complete rundown of what's available—and then ask for tomato juice or a Coke. The soft drinks and the juice are free; the alcohol and wine are usually not.

You've been given a menu to choose from—meat or sea-food. When the food cart reaches your row you should already have your table turned down and be ready to give your order. The flight attendant is trained to be polite but is not like a maître d' at your favorite restaurant. There's no use trying to chat about the relative merits of the two dishes that are offered. The attendant might not like either one. But that's a secret.

Once you receive your tray you should proceed with prudence. Unfold your paper napkin, locate the salt and pepper packets, and observe that, if your utensils are made of plastic, a little too much leverage on the knife or fork will break them. When you are finished, prepare your tray for pick up and leave it on the table. The attendants will be by in a while to fill your cup with coffee or tea.

With the major event of eating out of the way, we can feel the atmosphere of the plane changing. Becoming a little more relaxed, calmer. The passengers have regained their equilibrium. Now begins the fight against boredom.

BATTLING BOREDOM

You have got an eight-or-more hour flight staring you in the face, and you haven't thought about what you are going to do. Read a bit, maybe sleep. It doesn't seem very long. After all, you routinely put in that much time at the office.

But being confined to a small seat for eight hours, with only a couple of bathroom breaks, has no relationship to your usual schedule. The hours spent on an international flight seem to drag by. To make the time pass quicker you should decide in advance how you are going to occupy yourself.

If you are a reader or a businessman with work to do you are lucky. Other seasoned international travelers organize their flight into blocks of time that include everything from knitting to writing letters. Paradoxically the worst thing you can do is sleep.

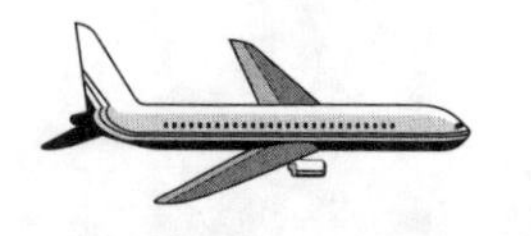

NAPPING FOR JET LAG

If you are dead tired, obviously you have no choice but to get some sleep. Many people try to sleep on planes, however, out of boredom, or because they think they are getting rest that will help energize them after they land. Wrong.

Most flights leave for Europe in the late evening. It's already morning in your new time zone. To sleep at your regular hours simply postpones your change to the new hours. You will find it helpful for your trip to take short naps on the plane, preparing your body by increments.

Actually it would be best to avoid sleeping at all and to take a two or three hour nap after you arrive at your hotel. Then to bed later, on your new schedule. But few people can manage that.

So now you have my suggestions for avoiding jet lag during the flight. In the best case, you won't eat—or you'll eat little. You won't sleep—or you'll sleep little. And you'll drink nothing but water.

Doesn't sound like much fun, I know. But it works. The fun starts after you land.

FLYING MANNERS

The young man who was seated in front of me on my recent flight—no, let me start over. The jerk in front looked like he was high on drugs. Before the plane had even taken off, he pulled a large sleeping mask over his face and jammed his seat back so far that I could barely move.

The attractive young woman who was sitting next to the jerk was deaf and unable to talk. (I'm not making this up.) I could see that she desperately wanted to go to the bathroom. But what could she do? She was blocked in by the jerk and she couldn't communicate with him. And she definitely did not want to touch his inert body to try to get his attention. She looked back at me several times, helplessly, hoping I would do something.

The younger me would've probably taken immediate action. But the older me waited until I could muster the support of several other passengers to roust the jerk so the woman could get out. I could only hope that she had a strong bladder.

Incidents like this are all too common these days, as manners decline worldwide. Sometimes, though, bad manners are inadvertent, because the person simply doesn't realize how he or she is unnecessarily irritating a fellow passenger.

Zalin Grant

There are several rules to good flying manners.

First, don't jam your knees into the seat in front of you. You are making the passenger uncomfortable. And this act of discourtesy, which on the face of it seems relatively insignificant, carries an irritant factor large enough to make some people's blood boil.

In the same manner, don't slam your table into the seat in front when you restore it to the normal position. Fold it up slowly and gently . And when you start to leave your seat don't grab the seat in front for leverage.

Your seat reclines. But it won't add appreciably to your comfort to push it back all the way. It will add considerably, though, to the discomfort of the passenger behind you.

The reading light is focused to shine directly down on your seat. But while the movie is being shown or during sleeping hours your light will irritate passengers who are sitting close by. Turn it off. Likewise, keep your window shade closed during sleeping hours. You might like bright sunshine. Most people won't.

The airlines could soundproof the airplane to make the cabin practically noiseless. But they don't. Because the engine noise masks and discourages loud conversation. Can you imagine a restaurant-like noise situation on a long flight? It would drive me crazy. Remember to keep your voice down.

THE LONG GLIDE

There is a stirring in the cabin. It starts with the attendants, freshly combed and perfumed, striding purposefully down the aisles. They are preparing for something. For what? Ah, the breakfast snack. It's a welcome sign that the flight is coming to an end. People begin to rush to the bathrooms. If you were flying smart you have already beat them there.

The descent of the aircraft to its landing pattern takes from twenty minutes to nearly an hour. You have plenty of time to prepare yourself. One thing you don't want to miss is your landing card. If you are an American citizen and traveling to Europe, you'll have to fill out the card and present it to immigration with your passport. So keep your eyes peeled for the attendant who's passing them out. Not everybody will need one. Citizens of the European Union are exempt. The card asks for your name, date of birth, permanent address, and number and name of your flight.

The cabin crew will retrieve the snack trays and earphones, pass out extra coffee and tea, and then ask that you fasten your seat belt and return your seat to the upright position.

Although you will notice some people do it, there is no use retrieving your carry-on from the overhead bin. You'll have plenty of time after the plane lands and comes to a complete stop.

Stay Seated

Some people are so anxious to get off the plane you would think they are about to climb out the windows as the aircraft taxis to its landing gate. The crew will make several appeals to remind everyone to stay in their seats. When it does finally jerk to a halt, minor chaos ensues, with everyone trying to retrieve their carry-ons and position themselves in the aisles to deplane. Of course there's no need to engage in this kind of bumping and pushing. But it seems to be the inevitable human reaction. I've never been on a flight when it did not occur.

Get in the Correct Line

You first must go through immigration control and show your passport and present your landing card. Look carefully at the signs over the immigration booths. Some will list European Union (EU) members only. That's not you. You're likely to fall into the "other" category. Enclose your landing card in your passport picture page and hand it to the immigration official when your turn comes.

If you are entering a European Union country and plan to travel later to one of seven others—that is, France, Germany, Spain, Portugal, Belgium, Holland, and Luxembourg—you may not be required to go through immigration and customs again. In theory, if you enter Spain by air and go through immigration checks there, you can drive to Amsterdam without being stopped a single time. Theory is not always put into practice, however.

When you are checked at immigration, just say a polite hello. This is not the time for further conversation on your part, except to answer any questions posed by the immigration official. Sometimes immigration agents ask to see the passenger's return ticket, so have it handy. Sometimes the agent will ask the purpose of your trip, business or pleasure. Answer straightforwardly and finish the immigration procedure as soon as possible.

THE MERRY-GO-ROUND

Some gremlin decreed many years ago that my bags would be near the last to be unloaded on every flight. Knowing there's no rush to pick up my luggage actually puts me in front of the game. Because I can focus on finding a baggage cart. That should be your first action. The carts disappear quickly after a major flight. Then you should carefully look at the signs on the various baggage carrousels to establish where your flight's luggage will appear. If you don't see a sign, ask a member of the airline's ground personnel. Don't waste time standing in the wrong pickup line.

HOW TO ACE CUSTOMS

If you are an American tourist and carrying only your personal belongings, you should not have any trouble going through foreign customs. Look for the "nothing to declare" line and walk through. Hold your passport in your left hand as you push your cart toward the exit, so customs officials can get a glance at it.

This had always worked for me until my recent flight back to Paris. The final customs official, who was from Martinique, stopped me when I was three feet from the exit.

"What do you have in there?" he demanded.

"Nothing but the tools of my trade, officer," I said, thinking about all the electronic gear I was bringing in.

"And what is your profession, monsieur?"

"Journalist and writer."

"C'est vrai? Wonderful. What do you think of the O.J. Simpson case?"

The customs official held me up so long to question me about the O.J. Simpson murder trial that Claude, who had come to pick me up, jumped through the one-way door, with the idea of saving me. She thought I was being arrested.

"What's the matter, officer?" Claude cried. "This man's my husband and I've got a flat tire."

"You've got what, Claude?" I cried.

"Well, if you've got a flat tire at Charles de Gaulle on a rainy afternoon, you had better be moving along," said the customs official sympathetically.

Sometimes flying smart is just not enough.

Beating U.S. Customs

How do I get through? I lie. Actually I lie because I don't really have anything to declare, and I'm afraid the customs officials won't believe me. As you will note on your travels the dollar is undervalued in many countries, so I purchase practically everything I need while I am in the States. Claude puts a couple of small gifts in my suitcase before I leave for my friends and family. But that's all I carry. Putting down the real—and insignificant—amount of my imports on the custom form has resulted in my baggage being opened and turned upside down on more than one occasion. So I write whatever I think will sound logical to customs officials. I'm careful of course to keep it well within the limit allowed.

I've never heard of anyone being punished for overstating how much they were bringing in. But I wouldn't recommend that you lie if you have gone over the limit. I think it's rather silly that once-a-year tourists are examined so closely, to see if they are a few dollars over their limit, while the U.S. blithely runs up a multi-billion dollar trade deficit with other countries. But that's the way it is. So fill out your customs form correctly.

If you are worried about customs questioning the value of a couple of your gifts, the best response is not to look worried. When you approach the customs counter you should not appear at all reluctant to open your luggage for inspection. In fact, you should start opening without the customs agent asking you to do it.

Yep. A little psych. It might work or might not. But it's your best chance. A show of reluctance will get you inspected every time.

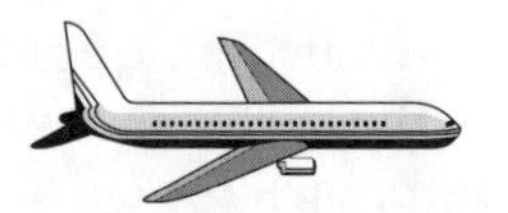

LEAVING THE AIRPORT

This is another confusing period for passengers. And a time when a lot of unnecessary mistakes are made. First, take a deep breath and collect yourself for a moment. It's not necessary to be the first in the taxi line or on the bus. There are a lot of hustlers circling around airports. And you want to make sure you don't get hooked up with one—no matter how attractive the proposed price looks. If you are at a major European airport and on a budget, I suggest you consider public transportation as a way of reaching town. The bus and train services from the airports have little in common with comparable American services. That's to say, they are efficient, clean, and reasonably priced.

If you plan to taxi into town, ignore all gypsy cabs or limos and find yours in the line of officially marked vehicles. It's a wonderful idea to learn at least a little of a country's language before you arrive. But this is not the time to practice. Carefully print the address where you are headed and give it to the taxi driver. The taxi will charge you the meter rate and sometimes an additional amount for each bag placed in the trunk.

If you think you are being cheated or taken advantage of, I suggest that you not try to argue while you are en route to your destination. Note the name and number of your driver, and hop out at the hotel under the pretense of looking for change. Then ask the hotel employees to intercede in your behalf to get the matter straightened out.

LAGGING OUT

I have a final suggestion to friends to get them over jet lag as soon as possible. Instead of taking a nap immediately on arrival at your hotel, I suggest you spend an hour or so walking around your immediate neighborhood. This is not a sightseeing trip but rather an orientation visit to build your confidence that you know and feel comfortable in your new surroundings. This feeling will in turn be transmitted to your confused body. After your walk-around is the time for a restful shower or bath, followed by a two or three hour nap. Then arise and carry on with your schedule as though you are a native.

CULTURE SMART

I have a friend who was familiar with French restaurants in the United States. She particularly liked saucisson sandwiches in a baguette. The first time I took her to a café in Paris she ordered her sandwich and was dismayed when it arrived. There was *butter* on the bread with the saucisson. It wasn't, in her mind, really a French sandwich. And she was sitting in Paris.

That is culture shock. Things often turn out not to be the way one expects in another country. Or the country's people act in a manner that seems totally illogical to the American mind.

But, remember, there's another side to this story. Why, for example, do Americans meet and immediately start first-naming each other? Why do they brag about how big their steak is, rather than how it tastes? Why do they tend to talk so loudly? Why do American men treat a simple handshake as a test of manhood?

These things, and dozens of other aspects of the American character, which we take for granted, are incomprehensible to European and Asian tourists who visit the United States.

It's their version of culture shock.

I've seen a lot of American tourists who were unable to enjoy their trips because they couldn't overcome culture shock. They were terribly bothered and upset that the people of the country they were visiting just didn't act—well, they didn't act American. Or they didn't act or look, say, French, the way they thought the French were supposed to look and act.

My advice is to go with the flow. Many aspects of national character cannot be explained or understood in rational terms. These are aspects deeply embedded in history and tradition. Don't waste your time and mental energy dueling with culture shock. Observe and enjoy. Vive la différence!

BE A TOURIST

Some Americans, for reasons I've never quite understood, hate to be thought of as a tourist. I am a tourist and hope to remain one for the rest of my life. The first thing I do when I go to an unfamiliar city, whether I'm driving my car or not, is to jump on a tour bus so I can get an overview of the place I am visiting. Then I'll return by myself for a closer look.

I know a young woman who came to Paris with the idea of really mastering the city in a historical and modern sense. She approached it like a job. Every day she arose early and went sightseeing, getting back late after an exhausting day. At the end of six months she had to return to the States. And she admitted to me that she had not seen nearly everything she had set out to see.

She was still a tourist.

So see what you can in your available time period. Don't worry about whether you are super hip or merely an extraordinary/ordinary tourist.

Just enjoy it.

And hey, glance over your shoulder every now and then.

Why?

Because that might be me standing behind you.

You know, the guy who is asking the tourist guide all the obvious questions.

THANKS

I'd like to click my heels and salute the following: Philippe Muller, a specialist in international travel whose help was priceless; Deborah Palmer; my sister Thurma Dean and her husband, J. David Smith; Janice Terry and the tireless staff of Pythia Press. Also Wallace H. Terry II & III, Noah Marcus, Susan Harrigan, Chuckie Franklin, Billye and Cedric Jessup. And Jack Scovil, Sam Abt, Sally Palmer, Carlos Campbell; Patricia and John Paton Davies, George Sturrock, Millie and Ying-Ying Yung. Frank McCulloch, A.M. Secrest, and Mr. Ernest (Matheson). I'd like to remember my late father, Thurman B. Grant. And of course I want to thank my mother, Barbara Smith Grant, who made this book necessary—and Claude, who made it possible.

MERCI

Je voudrais remercier les personnes suivantes: Philippe Muller, spécialiste des voyages internationaux, dont l'aide a été sans prix; Roxane Dodote et Ricardo Davila pour leur professionnalisme hors pair; Henry Muller, mon conseiller en communication; Deborah Palmer, Annie Miccio Belaiche, Robert et Odile Zantain, Jeanette Boutillon, Lucien et Suzanne Pierre, Yves et Jocelyne Le Corre, Robert et Chantal Micaud. Je voudrais y associer le souvenir de mon Père, Thurman B. Grant, et aussi celui de Panou. Et bien sûr je veux remercier ma Mère, Barbara Grant, qui a rendu ce livre nécessaire, et Claude qui l'a rendu possible.

ABOUT THE AUTHOR

Zalin Grant has flown over a million miles on everything from shot-up helicopters to the U.S. presidential jet, and visited more than eighty countries. He is a former journalist for *Time* and *The New Republic*. His books include *Over the Beach*, the widely acclaimed account of U.S. pilots at war. He divides his time between Washington and Paris.